The Snowshoe Handbook

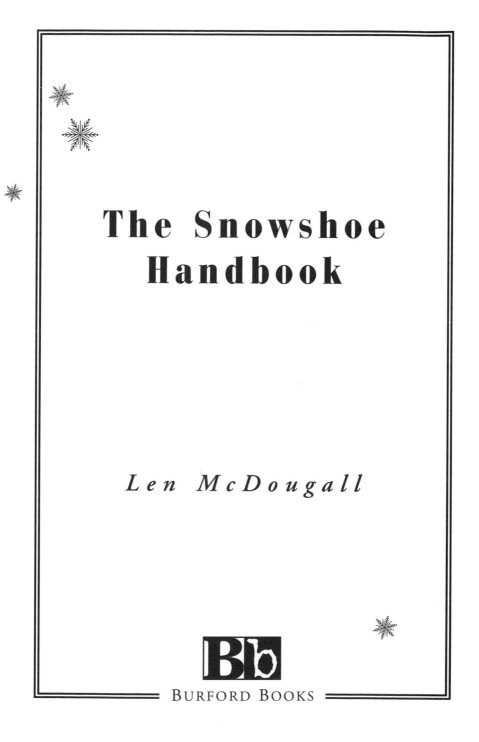

The Snowshoe Handbook

Len McDougall

Bb
BURFORD BOOKS

Printed in the United States of America

10 9 8 7 6 5 4 3 2 1

Library of Congress Cataloging-in-Publication Data

McDougall, Len.
    The snowshoe handbook / by Len McDougall.
        p. cm.
    Includes index.
    ISBN 1-58080-083-1 (pb)
     1. Snowshoes and snowshoeing. I. Title.

GV853 .M33 2000
796.9′2—dc21   00-040320

All illustrations have been supplied by the author except those noted below.

Chapter-opening photograph: Courtesy Tubbs Snowshoe Co., Vermont
Courtesy Great Bear Enterprises, Montana: 20, 21, 23, 24, 109
Courtesy Tubbs Snowshoe Co., Vermont: 26, 27, 116, 118
Courtesy Brunton: 79
Courtesy Tek-1: 91

Contents

This book is dedicated to Al, Archie,
and the biologists and staff of the Natural Resources
Commission of the Little Traverse Bay Bands of Odawa Indians.
Without their hard work the battle to save nature
would be much tougher, and this book
would have been less than it is.
Migwetch Anishnabe.

Preface

Not since the last ice age has there been a better time to be a snow-shoer. Having grown up in Northern Michigan B.C. (Before Condos), I've been snowshoeing almost as long as I've been walking, but until recently the allure of snow walking had been fading steadily. Racy multicolored snowmobiles provide a fast adrenaline rush with minimal physical exertion—their only drawbacks being that they're noxious, noisy, and tend to get stuck a lot in deep powder. Cross-country skis give folks with schedules to keep a quick way to enjoy some of the beauty of a snow-hushed forest, but skis don't do well for breaking trail through tangled brush. Despite those drawbacks, snowmobiling and cross-country skiing have long been the most popular winter sports; snowshoeing was too slow and too inconvenient for the rushed pace of civilized humans.

Still, there have always been a few snowshoers around, because in untracked wilderness snowshoes were and are the only truly reliable way of crossing deep snows that simply cannot be negotiated by any other means. With proper snowshoes you'll sink no more than 5–6 inches in the fluffiest powder, no matter how deep it might actually be, and you can negotiate almost any terrain. In fact, swamps and other places that are too gnarly to tackle in summer often become pleasant little treks when water becomes a solid and most obstacles are buried under hardpack. You can also carry considerable weight on a pair of snowshoes, which explains why snowshoeing has always been the preferred mode of winter travel for trappers of old and modern backpackers alike.

The problem was that until recent years snowshoes had remained mostly unchanged for half a millennium or more. The old rawhide lace-up binding was at best unstable between snowshoe and boot, requiring a learned toes-forward stride to keep the shoes "tracking" straight each time you moved one forward. Rawhide laces often stretched and needed retightening on the trail, traction was only fair, and some folks complained of sore feet at the end of the day. Despite their enduring utility for the few linemen, rangers, and trappers who still required them, snowshoes simply were too slow and inconvenient to suit modern outdoor lovers, who must budget their free time.

Today all of that has changed for the better—much better in some instances. Boots, gloves, and clothing are many times warmer, lighter, and more functional than anything available to previous generations. No one ever need get cold anymore, regardless of temperature, windchill, or exposure time. Some folks still do get cold, but given today's affordable high-efficiency insulations and materials, those few have no one to blame but themselves.

Although outdoor equipment has improved generally, no item of winter gear has undergone more of an evolution in recent years than have snowshoes. Just browsing through an outfitter store or catalog will reveal such a variety of snowshoes that someone out to purchase his first pair might easily develop a headache before making a decision. Worse, you might come away with a pair of snowshoes that aren't right for your intended use.

This book is meant to help everyone from first-timers to avid enthusiasts better enjoy the fine old sport of snow walking as it exists today. It begins with a brief history of how snowshoes were quite literally responsible for the global spread of humanity—our ancestors could never have left Africa without them. Following chapters will guide you through the nuts, bolts, thrills, and perils of traveling places where no machines and only few animals may go. You'll find sometimes hard-learned tips for making the transition from ground to snow as gracefully as possible, with field-proven suggestions for spotting potential hazards before you encounter them. You'll learn the secrets of dressing warmly for any weather, how to repair broken snowshoes in the field, and how to navigate when trails disappear beneath a white blanket. And just in case this book succeeds in making you want to tread the powder for yourself, I've included real-world evaluations of several of today's most popular snowshoe models.

Aside from the sheer beauty of a snow-hushed forest that's so utterly silent you can actually hear snowflakes fall, there are some truly practical benefits to be gained from recreational snowshoeing. For one, it's impossible to be a regular snowshoer without losing fat and getting into shape. A 'shoer following a packed trail on flat ground at the reckless pace of 2 miles per hour is burning upward of 7 calories a minute. Throw in steep hills, overgrown terrain, or a backpack, and that energy consumption might easily double or even triple. When you're snowshoeing, counting calories means making sure there are enough snacks in the daypack to keep your metabolic furnace stoked.

A respiratory therapist friend tells me snowshoeing is the kind of stamina-building exercise that actually burns cholesterol plaque from arterial walls, and he claims it can reduce the chance of coronary occlusion to almost zero if practiced enough. He also says that snowshoeing helps prevent emphysema by opening the lungs and working them to depths not normally reached in daily life.

Personally, I've found that regular snowshoeing trips seem to result in a much stronger immune system that seems to shrug off the onset of cold and flu viruses with just a good night's sleep. The same cardiovascular workout that digests arterial plaque and strengthens virtually every muscle also works to beef up a snowshoer's auto-immune system against all types of infectious organisms.

Despite all that exercise, snowshoeing is a no-impact sport that almost anyone can enjoy, young or old, big or small. You don't need to be an athlete (that comes with regular practice), and you don't need any special skills. You don't even need a lot of money; a decent pair of beginner's 'shoes costs about $60, though you'll probably want to upgrade if snowshoeing gets into your blood. With a good pair of snowshoes and warm clothing, all that remains is a desire to see vistas and sights that no nonsnowshoer can ever witness. Better take your camera.

I must also admit to having an entirely selfish reason for wanting more folks to take up snowshoeing. It is no exaggeration to say that our natural world is right now dying, caught in a death grip by its most successful progeny. Groundwaters are undrinkable, rivers are infested with flesh-eating bacteria, and timber companies are paying top dollar for "garbage" wood they wouldn't have condescended to cut less than a generation ago. An estimated 50 million tons of sulfuric acid exhaust is pumped into the atmosphere yearly by American cars alone. The air in some cities is so toxic that radio stations carry public service warnings against breathing on certain days. Native freshwater fish species have been and are being decimated by destructive ocean life dumped into the Great Lakes from the bilgewater of shipping lines that make Exxon look responsible. Frogs are dying from increased UV levels, and American whitetails are dying from bovine tuberculosis. Kids in Australia are required by law to wear long pants and a hat to school, while global corporations rent experts to tell us that a growing hole in the ozone layer is normal. There are innumerable environmental controversies that we can't afford to ignore or to be wrong about. But until those who care enough to act outnumber those who don't, corporate politicians and hair-splitting lawyers will continue to kill this planet for the sake of a bottom line.

I don't believe anyone can spend time surrounded by nature without developing a love for the very things mankind has spent so much energy trying to erase with golf courses, condominiums, and a seemingly endless demand for new houses. My admittedly selfish reason for writing this book is simply to get more folks into the winter woods. If you once experience a snow-locked wilderness where only a snowshoer may roam with impunity, I'm betting that you'll love it. If you love it, you'll want to see it protected, and that alone is a great big step in the right direction.

1

A History of Snowshoes

If anthropologists are correct, humankind originated on the continent of Africa during the Pleistocene age, 3.5 to 5.5 million years ago. They tell us that humans began as a small apelike prey animal known as *Australopithecus,* then evolved to *Homo habilis* (handy man), and finally to *Homo erectus* (upright man). By 4000 B.C. our common ancestors are thought to have spread from Africa to Europe and Asia, and from there across a land bridge that once spanned the snow-locked Bering Straits to North America. Early humans who remained in Africa developed a slender, hairless physique in response to their warm habitat, and became known as Anatomically Modern *Homo sapiens.* Those who walked out of Africa into the cold evolved a more hairy and more burly physique, also attributed to environmental conditions, and became known as Archaic *Homo sapiens,* or simply as Neanderthal man.

Since any trek out of Africa almost certainly meant going north into a climate not always favorable to hairless bipeds, those

Snowshoes come in an impressive variety of styles and shapes.

first pilgrims had to learn how to cope with cold and snow, including country-sized glaciers and at least one ice age. Clothing fashioned from the hides of animals dressed more warmly than themselves allowed nomadic tribes to travel in cold that would have otherwise killed them, while mastery of fire made life in winter at least survivable.

But deep snows have always presented a more or less impassable obstacle for bipedal humans, especially while bearing the weight of game and fish or migrating with the necessities of life to warmer climes. As anyone who's ever tried it can verify, slogging through waist-deep powder is quite literally heartbreaking exertion; add a thin frozen crust to that snow's surface and it becomes impossible to traverse on foot.

But by wearing crude, heavy snowshoes fashioned from pliable green wood and decked with a web of interwoven bark or rawhide, early humans found they could walk atop deep snow, even while carrying a load. With that discovery ours became the only species capable of carrying food, shelter, and other trappings of life with it during a migration. That and an already established mastery of fire gave *Homo sapiens* the means to cross or even live in places too hostile for many other forms of wildlife. Soon, virtually no place was so inhospitable that the unique paired tracks of humans couldn't be found. Ours had become the dominant species on planet earth.

ANIMAL SNOWSHOES

Deep snows are a real hardship to most wildlife species, especially hooved animals. Edible ground plants die or are buried, leaving herbivores with a poor, almost nutritionless starvation diet of buds, bark, and twigs until warm weather returns. To survive until spring, predator and prey alike must take in enough food calories to keep their metabolic furnaces stoked. The colder it gets, the more they need to eat (just like a snowshoer), and animals that don't take in enough calories to keep their body temperatures up are in genuine danger of freezing to death.

Winter is not cruel, in spite of uniquely human sensibilities, but it can be unforgiving of physical frailties in any life-form not sufficiently prepared to endure it—a truism that every snowshoer should take to heart. In every species the old and weak are the first to die or be killed by predators, their carcasses used to feed other species that range from mammals and birds to insects and plant life. Pregnant mothers not sufficiently well fed or healthy at the start of winter will spontaneously abort their fetuses, an almost universal and completely natural phenomenon that reserves all available energies for a weakened female's survival.

Deep snows compound this harsh environment, restricting the travel of most land animals not hibernating to a fraction of what it had been in warmer months, and further limiting the availability of precious foods. March finds many species gaunt and starving, with fat reserves gone and their bodies now cannibalizing muscle tissue for the nutrition needed to survive until spring. In the latter stages of starvation a victim's remaining muscle mass becomes toxic, foul to the taste buds as well as the stomach, and only scavenging birds or the most starved of carnivores will eat it.

But every nonhibernating species in snow country has also adapted in some degree to life in the fourth season. Members of the deer family have long legs to keep their heavy bodies from dragging in snow, although most "yard" together all winter long in protected places where wind and snow are minimal. Otters use their short legs and long supine bodies to leap, slide, and even tunnel through powder with surprising agility. A porcupine uses its broad, flat belly as a toboggan, sliding over top of the deepest powder propelled by short, stout legs and large feet.

But the lynx and the aptly named snowshoe hare are probably nature's best examples of animals that have evolved large, snowshoelike feet to keep them atop winter hardpack. Both have comparatively large feet and long legs that provide excellent flotation on deep powder, giving them the ability to spring hard against and run atop snow too soft to support lesser-footed animals. So closely matched and interdependent are these two snow runners that a decline in the population of one in a given environment will have an equal impact on the other one year later.

MANKIND'S FIRST SNOWSHOES

Probably taking a cue from the animals he hunted and competed with for food, one day a common ancestor came upon the realization that larger feet are the secret to walking over deep snows. With that understanding, a creativity unmatched by other species, and long fingers well adapted for fashioning tools, that ancestor created artificial platforms that tied to human feet.

While other species had evolved to cope with snow, ours was the first to immediately create its own means of walking atop deep powder from the surrounding environment. Tools fashioned from stone, wood, and rawhide had already been in use for millennia, but the invention of snowshoes represented a huge milestone in human creativity.

Early records describe snowshoes framed with springy green saplings, like willow and cedar, that were bent into a teardrop shape then tied together at the tails and decked with interwoven strips of bark, pliable twigs, or rawhide. Bindings were simply leather thongs or braided rope that tied the snowshoes to their wearer's feet.

Probably the first manufactured snowshoe was a model known as the Ojibwa, which is described in greater detail in chapter 2. Ingenious in its simplicity, the canoe-shaped Ojibwa frame is essentially just two bowed pieces of wood lashed together at each end and held apart in the center by wooden crosspieces. Ojibwa snowshoes could be manufactured quickly from most winter environments, giving whole tribes an unmatched ability to migrate away from cold climes even after many other animals had become snowbound.

Later came the technology to steam hardwoods, especially ash, making them pliable enough to bend without splintering. With essentially the same methods used today, a steam-softened frame was placed onto a "jig," a flat board with perpendicular pegs to hold the bent wood in a desired shape as it cooled. Primitive humans had nothing comparable to modern decking fabrics, but they had plenty of rawhide strips with which to make a webbing inside the snowshoe frame. Rawhide was, and still is, one of toughest, most pliable, yet long-lived decking materials, and only since the computer age has it been finally replaced with synthetic fabrics.

SNOWSHOES AND
THE SPREAD OF HUMANITY

With snowshoes that provided better flotation on the deepest snow than any other animal enjoyed, the spread of humanity was not only possible but inevitable. Fire, the first element to be bent to human will, had removed our kind from the food chain, while an ability to manufacture lethal weapons from any environment made nomadic tribes much too formidable to be considered worthwhile prey. If our earliest human ancestors had ever been the regular diet of large carnivores, as some anthropologists suggest, they certainly weren't anymore. Even the large and decidedly man-eating polar bear was intimidated by a group of Inuit hunters armed with spears and arrows, just as African lions have learned to flee at the approach of Masai tribesmen.

Early hunters and pilgrims on snowshoes could invade the most snowbound environments, across places that were impassable during warmer seasons. They would have found yarded deer, moose, elk, and buffalo relatively easy prey during the snowiest winter months. Ironically, snowshoes provided slow and mostly senseless humans with the only chance they could have of running down large game on its own turf.

One trick employed by American Indians on snowshoes was to purposely chase whitetails, moose, bison, or elk into deep snow or onto glare ice, where the floundering animals could be safely and easily caught. Cornered through exhaustion and effectively disarmed, large game could then be dispatched quickly at close range—the only range available to hunters whose weapons were stone-tipped spears and arrowheads. Large kills were sledded to camp on bark toboggans, but a lone trapper running a line of snares on snowshoes could carry a quartered yearling whitetail without much strain (I've done it a few times).

In Europe, where large cities and established roads have existed since recorded history, skis were a natural offshoot of snowshoes. Snowshoes did exist there, like the squarish all-wood Swedish variation, but regular commerce between communities and the farms that fed them demanded faster modes of transport that could haul larger loads. Wide, hard-packed roads were established, allowing the citizenry to ski quickly between neighbors and towns in winter, and to transport very heavy cargo with horse-drawn sleighs.

But there were no roads in the New World. Hauling heavy loads through the rugged, untracked forests of northern America demanded the flotation and stability of snowshoes. As evidenced by their dogsleds and sledges, American Indians were aware of the concept of skis, and of the wheel, but neither was an advantage without roads. A hunter stalking the thick cover of a winter white-tail yard needed the flotation and agility of snowshoes as much as the same hunter laboring under 50 pounds of quartered venison on the return trip.

Oddly, snowshoes were never used much in the Far North, which explains why one rarely sees an Inuit on them. Snow at or above the tundra line in winter is typically very dense and kept rock hard by temperatures that some might describe as bitterly cold. Once a hardpack layer has settled, this snow will support a half-ton moose, so a human passing over it will barely leave a mark. Snowshoes are more a hindrance than a help on such hardened snow.

SNOWSHOES IN MODERN TIMES

In the winter of 1997 more than a hundred motorists died in their cars when a heavy snowstorm blanketed interstate expressways across Ohio, Indiana, and Illinois. I sat up late that night listening to impersonal newscasters announce each increase in the death toll like electronic grim reapers. Once a line of vehicles had been stalled by snow the freeway became a trap, bringing all traffic to a halt. Snowplows couldn't get through, and attempts to evacuate stuck motorists by snowmobile proved mostly futile in the deep, loose powder snow of a blizzard. I've never been able to shake the vision of folks dying in the imagined safety of their cars, perhaps within sight of a towering lighted gas station sign but unable to reach it through blowing and drifted snow.

Even today, despite all our technology, snowshoes remain the most reliable method of crossing snow of any depth or consistency in any type of terrain. Modern cross-country skis are great on groomed trails, but the best of them suffer from lack of flotation and an ungainly design not well suited to negotiating underbrush. Smart cross-country skiers carry the means to survive an unplanned night in the woods, but few attempt to carry a full-size (50-plus pounds) backpack, and fewer try it twice. A winter backpacker who breaks trail cross-country and stays out for several days is a snowshoer because he must be, just as every northern trapper once had to be a snowshoer.

Snowmobiles also do well on established trails, but when the snow is deep and drifted, or the trail unbroken, their tracks tend to dig in on one side, causing the machine to bog down and get stuck frequently. A 600-pound snowmobile cannot safely break trail over frozen marshes, where snowed-under shrubs may support a foot of seemingly smooth hardpack over hollows that can send rider and machine crashing down 2 feet or more. Snow machines are too wide to negotiate the thickly forested places where snowshoers roam at will, and despite improvements in reliability snowmobiles can still break down in the backcountry. Too, adding a quarter ton to your own body weight changes the definition of *safe ice* entirely, and misjudging ice strength over open water is something you might get to do just one time.

As the blizzard described earlier illustrates only too well, snow-mobilers, motorists, or any folks spending time in snow country are well advised to consider snowshoes a necessary tool in both home and car. In recent years winter storms have come to rank as some of the most lethal natural catastrophes in America, and too many fatalities have resulted because a victim simply gave out from exhaustion, then hypothermia, before reaching safety. With good snowshoes in the trunk, strapped to your snowmobile, or hanging on the cabin wall, you're free to travel with impunity in any snow, no matter how deep. If all those poor folks stranded on the inter-state had been carrying snowshoes, they could have evacuated themselves far more efficiently than the authorities did.

Modern snowshoes, even traditional styles, are better than ever, and there are dozens of models in as many price ranges to give snowshoers plenty of options. Some are made for racing, some for dayhiking, and some for backpacking. Traditional Native American styles are still being made in many of their original configurations. Chapter 2 deals more specifically with the assortment of styles and types of snowshoes available to those wishing to try this most ancient—and still most effective—mode of winter transportation.

With good snowshoes you're free to travel with impunity in any snow, no matter how deep.

2

Snowshoeing Today

Snowshoeing today is in many ways exactly the same as it was when the first human pilgrims crossed the frozen northern wastes to settle in Europe, Asia, and the Americas. Snow and cold haven't changed, even though equipment and clothing for dealing with them have improved drastically in recent years. There have always been avalanches in steep terrain, and blizzards can still blind travelers to anything more than a few feet distant. Waist-deep drifts are still impossible to walk through, and when a hard, wind-driven storm front closes all major highways across whole states to travel, a snowshoer can still know the real meaning of total isolation.

But snowshoeing has also changed in many ways, and some of the most important changes have been applied to the snowshoes themselves. Modern synthetics and tooling have done for snowshoes what cartridge ammunition did for firearms, and even handcrafted traditional-style snowshoes have benefited from advancements in materials and tooling.

There are as many options and features as there are models. The advantage is that you can get closer to selecting precisely the right snowshoe because there are so many options among which to choose. The downside is that as snowshoe manufacturing has become more competitive, more innovative ideas are becoming features. The resulting array of models, designs, and proprietary nomenclature is sufficient to give even experienced snowshoers a headache, and all of those keep changing every year.

But there are basic features that should be considered generic to every snowshoe, even though one method of doing something might not look like another company's design. Before you can make an informed selection about which snowshoe will best suit your needs, you need to be familiar with the generics of snowshoe anatomy and function. Otherwise you could end up at the mercy of a salesclerk who might see you simply as a buyer for snowshoes that have been in stock too long.

HOW SNOWSHOES WORK

Snowshoes keep their wearer afloat, so to speak, because each 'shoe has a surface area several times that of the wearer's foot. As a result, a snowshoer's body weight is more broadly distributed over a greater surface area, meaning that substantially less weight per square inch is being exerted downward with snowshoes than without them. The reason a snowshoer can walk atop snow that won't support the weight of a human on foot is because as far as snow is concerned, a snowshoer weighs less.

All things being equal, the more space a snowshoe covers, the more weight it will hold up on snow. A general rule of thumb for determining how much weight a 'shoe can carry on hardpack trail is 1 pound per 1 square inch. Thus a 9"×30" general-duty 'shoe can be expected to hold a snowshoer weighing 270 pounds or less; subtract 25 percent of that value if the snow is powdery or the trail unbroken. If the number you calculate is less than the number of pounds your snowshoes will be expected to carry, go to a bigger 'shoe. This rule isn't precise, but it's probably more reliable than manufacturer ratings, which can vary as much as 30 pounds from one company to another for same-sized snowshoes.

BINDINGS

Bindings are the connection between your foot and its snowshoe, and how well you like snowshoeing will have a lot to do with how well your bindings do their jobs. Poor bindings can allow the snowshoe to move laterally as you step, the result being that your

Modern snowshoe bindings such as these are a huge improvement over past designs.

weight comes down diagonally across the shoe, instead of in its center. That can cause one side of the snowshoe to sink deeper than the other, throwing you off balance, and it's a decidedly irritating way to snowshoe. If you don't fall over, being off balance all the time will get old fast, as will the constant clacking of your snowshoe frames hitting together.

In most instances with most bindings, the best procedure for mounting them to your boot is as follows: First position the toe of the boot forward enough to place the binding's main support (a toeplate on some newer models) under the ball of your foot, but rearward far enough to clear the snowshoe's forward decking. Once your foot is in place and straight on the 'shoe, tighten the binding, beginning at the toe. When the instep laces or straps are snug and straight across your boot, fasten the binding's heel strap to lock

If you can't seem to get a pair of snowshoes straight on your feet, try reversing them.

everything in place. Properly mounted, the snowshoes should drop smoothly at their tails when the foot is raised.

If you just can't seem to get a pair of snowshoes straight on your feet, try reversing them. With a few exceptions, most bindings have a left and a right, a fact that should be stated in their owner's manuals. If you don't have the manual, wear your snowshoes in the way that looks and feels best, because the difference between left and right is usually apparent as soon as you start walking. Probably most bindings are designed buckles-out, but some might be buckles-in, a few buckles-up, and older styles may have no buckles at all. You might need to experiment with a new or unfamiliar pair of snowshoes to determine which is left and right.

Lace-up leather bindings, like those on my old bearpaws, have probably been responsible for discouraging more folks from snowshoeing than the cold. Laces can be all but impossible to manipulate with gloved hands, they tend to stretch or come loose at the most inopportune times, and rawhide is especially prone to freezing stiff. If your traditional-style 'shoes came with rawhide laces, I recommend replacing them with good synthetic bootlaces of as large a diameter as you can find.

A problem common to all the bindings I've worn is that of ice buildup and freezing. One of the last things a tired snowshoer wants to do at the end of a hard day is fight to get his snowshoes off. Yet ice-caked buckles, straps, and lacing can make removing a pair of snowshoes much tougher than putting them on had been.

The cure for frozen bindings is to make them as water repellent as possible, because no water means no ice. For leather and neoprene, I use an application of ordinary silicone spray, available for around $5 in the automotive section of most department stores. Silicone not only provides long-lasting water repellency to prevent freezing, but it also helps keep leather and neoprene from aging and cracking. But always remember that silicone is extremely slippery stuff. Never apply it in any area where you might need traction.

Silicone spray also works well on nylon-strap types, but I prefer to saturate woven materials with Liquid NikWak, the same stuff I use on my pac and hiking boots. Both have long-lasting water-repellent properties that help keep moisture from collecting and freezing on straps and buckles, but NikWax seems to remain in the fabric longer, and it isn't so darned slippery. Conventional boot greases and oils are a last resort because they always wash away, but all types of binding harnesses should receive some type of water-repellent treatment.

If your trail takes you across marsh and swampland, you might find it useful to treat the toes and tails of your snowshoes with silicone as well. The ground under a swamp is seldom frozen; flowing springs and heat generated by constant, if retarded, decomposition work to create pockets of mucky water under apparently solid hardpack. I've often had my snowshoe tracks fill with water over marshland, even though ambient temperatures were well below freezing and several feet of hardpack lay on the ground.

Having your snowshoes sink under several inches of water is reason enough to be wearing a quality pair of waterproof snow pacs, but the most annoying result is a buildup of ice that can double, even triple the weight of each snowshoe. Silicone works well to prevent ice from forming on decks and frames, and it helps protect both from aging prematurely. Never apply silicone or wax to the bottoms of your snowshoes, and be careful not to get the slippery stuff any place your boot soles make contact. My preferred method of application is to spray silicone onto a cloth, then wipe it only onto the sections of decking I want to remain ice-free.

SNOWSHOEING POLES AND STAFFS

Many snowshoers employ one or two ski-type poles in a kind of outrigger system that helps them keep their balance on uneven terrain. Poles can be helpful on steep grades because they provide what is essentially a handhold that permits the upper body to assist in climbing. Most cross-country skiers who snowshoe for exercise also like that poles help them to maintain a familiar gait and pace.

Poles aren't needed with newer crampon-type bindings, but hills and rough country are most easily handled with the support of poles when you're wearing less aggressive 'shoes. Adding upper-body strength into the effort of climbing a steep grade on non-crampon snowshoes greatly decreases the amount of sometimes hazardous backsliding that occurs.

Better for me personally is having both hands unencumbered, especially when breaking trail in thick cover. In those places where snow covers then builds onto springy willows and dogwoods, I've had large areas of hardpack suddenly give way under me. The fall isn't usually far—no more than 2 feet or so— but it can send an unwary snowshoer toppling over into trees, and sometimes there's standing water under those hollows. The good part is that places where such things happen will usually offer many saplings and trees to grab if you lose your balance. But you need to have your hands free to do that. If you feel more secure with poles, by all means use them, but they aren't required equipment.

TRADITIONAL SNOWSHOE STYLES

Like mukluk boots, brass compasses, and union-suit long underwear with a trapdoor in the back, there still exists a strong romantic attraction to traditional wooden-frame snowshoes like those worn by Indians and trappers of old. I wore traditional snowshoes for more than two decades and in all honesty I prefer the aggressive traction and strength of newer models.

Still, I have to admit to a certain tendency toward buckskin and Indian-style mukluks when I'm snow walking on rawhide (or neoprene) and wood. I can imagine the spirits of long-dead generations of voyageurs, soldiers, and Indians with me when I wear my old bearpaws along the same routes they once used to transport game, pelts, and trade goods.

Most traditional snowshoes are framed with white ash, the wood of choice, and decked with crisscross lacings of rawhide or neoprene. The majority are as lightweight as their manufactured counterparts, despite a commonly held belief that synthetic 'shoes are lighter, and many are built for hauling heavy loads. Flotation is almost as good as that of synthetic-decked snowshoes, even though the web-type decking of traditional designs might make it appear otherwise.

Downsides include a tendency for toes to chip, then splinter against trees in rough country. One of the first things I do to protect a pair of wooden-frame snowshoes is to encase the toe of the frame inside a wrapped bumper of cloth safety tape. Web decking provides good traction, but the short "ice claws" sometimes found on older 'shoes provide nowhere near the braking and holding action of newer designs. Bindings are often primitive and not very secure, allowing shoes to shift diagonally underfoot and requiring a learned stride to keep the snowshoes tracking straight behind their wearer (see chapter 3).

The worst problem with wooden-frame shoes, and one that

I've seen twice, is that "bridging" the frames across two solid objects, like fallen trees or rocks, can exert enough force against the frame to snap it in half. Bridging is seldom a problem on established trails, but in the frozen swamplands and deadfalls where the only trails are your own it should be a constant concern. One broken snowshoe means no snowshoes at all, and that by itself can have real consequences when miles of deep powder lay between civilization and yourself.

Because they are still mostly handcrafted, there are as many variations as there are builders of traditional snowshoes, but all are descended from four basic models: Michigan, bearpaw, Ojibwa, and Alaska. Each of these is available in its original form, but many modern traditional-style 'shoes alter or modify the classic lines for reasons of improvement or propriety. For now we'll start by covering the basic, original snowshoe designs.

MICHIGAN

Easily the most recognizable snowshoe design, the tennis-racket-shaped Michigan, or Maine, snowshoe was less popular in the rolling hills and tangled swamps of Michigan than it was on the flat northern plains. Created in an era of simple and comparatively unstable bindings, the Michigan's intentionally heavy long tails are designed to drag behind in the snow with each step. Being tail heavy helps keep the shoes tracking in line with their wearer's feet. This was a useful feature for heavily laden Indians crossing the wide, flat northern plains in search of wintering bison and elk, but the Michigan's long tails pose a real tripping hazard in undergrowth. Catching a tail between two saplings is common, sometimes levering the wearer off balance and over—very hazardous along overgrown and undercut riverbanks. Another constant con-

Michigan, or Maine, snowshoes, also known as Hurons. Courtesy Great Bear Enterprises.

cern in forest is that the Michigan's tails are so easily bridged across logs and other high points.

First-time Michigan wearers nearly always complain that the snowshoes are too wide, forcing them to walk bowlegged. Narrower variations help remedy that, usually at the cost of flotation, but if you place a pair of classic working-sized Michigans side by side, they do indeed force you to stand spraddle legged.

The secret to walking in Michigans and other wide snowshoes is to "nest" them with each step. That is, position the inside frames against one another until their combined width is as narrow as possible. For the Michigan that means fitting the outward radius of the rear snowshoe's toe into the inward-curved tail radius of the forward 'shoe. Nesting means that you need to keep your legs spread only half as wide as they'd need to be if the snowshoes were directly side by side, which is much less tiring.

Different lengths and widths of snowshoes require a different stride lengths to get the two nested properly, so before purchasing or renting any conventional wood-and-leather snowshoe, try it on. Because they are designed to nest while walking, different frame lengths and curvatures represent different stride lengths; try to select a snowshoe whose stride matches your own as closely as possible. Too short a stride and you'll be "baby-stepping"; too long a stride and you'll be stretching with every step. Either takes a lot of the fun out of snowshoeing.

BEARPAW

This has always been my favorite among traditional wood-and-leather snowshoes, because it's the workhorse. I've since retired

Bearpaw snowshoes. Courtesy Great Bear Enterprises.

them to a place of honor on my wall, but my old rawhide-laced bearpaws, stamped with the year 1945 on their white ash frames, served reliably for nearly half a century. I ran traplines on them, wore them ice fishing, and trekked to the general store for baby formula when snow made the roads impassable even to snowmobiles. I learned at an early age to prize my bearpaws as a necessary household survival item in snow country.

Like other conventional-style snowshoes, traditional bearpaws suffer from a real lack of traction on steep grades, despite so-called ice claws on mine. Bindings are typically primitive and somewhat unstable, requiring a conscious toes-forward pace to keep the snowshoes tracking straight. In deep unbroken powder the bearpaw's width makes it notorious for sinking more deeply on one side—usually the outside—instead of straight down and flat. This has never posed a problem for me, though I think it worth mentioning, and the tipping problem becomes less pronounced when the bearpaw is placed under a stout load, as it was meant to be.

The bearpaw's advantages are also numerous. Rounded egg-shaped frames slide around rather than catching against half-buried obstacles, while the compact design provides good maneuverability in thick brush. Bearpaws are short enough to carry tied to a backpack, and only the Michigan can match their ability to support heavy loads on loose snow.

OJIBWA

Probably the most unconventional of traditional snowshoe styles, the canoe shape of an Ojibwa-style snowshoe is more functional than you might think at first glance. Simple frame design

Ojibwa snowshoes. Courtesy Great Bear Enterprises.

made it easy to construct from most shrubs and trees in almost any winter environment, which is by itself a desirable quality.

Used extensively by the Odawa and its namesake Ojibwa tribes, this snowshoe's pointed, upturned ends make it an outstanding performer in heavy untracked undergrowth, slipping between and dividing brush like a knife. Because the classic canoe shape is also upturned at the rear (some newer models are rounded), the Ojibwa style lends itself well to stepping backward, something most other snowshoe designs can do only with difficulty.

Flotation is less with the Ojibwa than with comparable bearpaw or Michigan models, but it was never intended to carry the heavy loads of those workhorse designs. Instead, the Ojibwa is best known for its ability to carry a fast-moving and lightly equipped hunter into the tangled winter browsing grounds of deer, rabbits, and other game.

ALASKA

The Alaska snowshoe is a happy medium between the bearpaw and Ojibwa styles. Shaped much like a bearpaw that has been stretched from both ends, the Alaska is narrower, flat sided, and more forgiving of different stride lengths than Michigan or bearpaw designs. That means it will accommodate a wide range of wearers and leg lengths, which makes the Alaska a favorite rental model. Most modern backcountry snowshoe designs use the Alaska as their model.

As its name suggests, the Alaska is a popular snowshoe in northwestern Canada and Alaska's interior, where windswept hardpack means greater snow density and less need for flotation than on powder. A long and narrow design makes the 'shoes tail heavy and helps them track well across bumpy hardpack.

The Alaska is also a popular model with many rabbit hunters

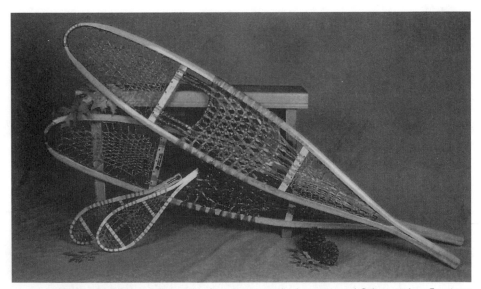

Alaska snowshoes, a happy medium between the bearpaw and Ojibwa styles. Courtesy Great Bear Enterprises.

around Northern Michigan, where I live. Like most ash-and-rawhide shoes, traction is provided by the deck webbing, so the design performs less than optimally on steep grades. But with secure bindings, the Alaska can break trail through overgrown cedar swamp with the best of them.

Interesting variations on the Alaska that I haven't yet field-tested are Tubbs's Traditional Series bearpaw models, whose elongated designs actually make them less bearpaw than Alaska. Framed in white ash and decked with rawhide webbing, both the 9"×30" bearpaw ($200) and the 10"×36" Green Mountain bearpaw ($205) come fitted with Tubbs's crampon-type TD-91 binding for solid braking and traction on steep grades. The smaller bearpaw weighs 4.9 pounds per pair and is rated to carry 160 pounds; the Green Mountain bearpaw will support up to 200 pounds with a pair weight of 5 pounds.

MODERN SNOWSHOE STYLES

If you're an adventurous type for whom part of the appeal of snowshoeing is an ability to leave the beaten path and explore places that can be seen no other way, a modern synthetic snowshoe is probably best suited to your needs. None of this latest generation of metal-and-fabric snow-walking footwear can have the same nostalgia or hand-finished beauty of a handcrafted wooden-frame snowshoe, but the difference in backcountry performance can be remarkable. Just as skis have evolved from rough wooden slats that tied to their wearer's feet, so too have snowshoes benefited from new technology.

Details about specific models of modern snowshoes are given in chapter 8, but most offer several advantages over old-style shoes. Bindings are nearly always crampon type, with quick-release nylon

The Tubbs Piranha aerobic snowshoe—a modern design for the snow jogger.

straps for sure footing even on glare ice and more or less glove-friendly operation. Tubular aluminum frames found on most models provide unsurpassed strength and flexibility, while nearly indestructible synthetic fabric decking materials provide about 20 percent more flotation than conventional webbing. Traditional snowshoes are every bit as good today as they ever were, but if you need a hard-core backcountry 'shoe for busting trail through the gnarly stuff, I'd suggest a synthetic model.

SNOWSHOES FOR KIDS

If snowshoeing is a great winter activity for adults, it's just what the doctor ordered for rambunctious kids with a dose of cabin fever. No child is hyperactive on snowshoes—at least not for

The Tubbs "Tubbscout" children's snowshoe. Courtesy Tubbs Snowshoe.

Kids usually have as much fun on snowshoes as adults—or more.

more than a few minutes—and the activity is just as beneficial to young growing bodies as it is to older arthritic ones like mine. The real payoff is that youngsters who take a shine to 'shoeing and do it regularly may avoid getting sick from a cold or flu all winter because their immune systems are peaked.

Snowshoes for children are a relatively new invention. It wasn't lack of desire that kept me from snowshoeing until I was 12, but lack of size. Like rifles, chain saws, and tractors, the snowshoes of a generation ago required a youngster to grow into them; the kids' shoes that were available then were specially made and more for novelty than serious use.

Today kids can take their pick of a variety of snowshoes made just for them. Parents can get their toddlers on snowshoes sooner than they can get them onto a potty, and for less money than a trip to the pediatrician. Kids usually have as much fun on snowshoes as adults—or more—and snowshoeing seems a far saner approach to dealing with natural youthful exuberance than Ritalin.

3

Snowshoeing Techniques

One of the best things about learning to snowshoe in modern times is that virtually anyone with a working pair of legs can set out over the hardpack as soon as his bindings are tight. That includes children as young as two years, older folks with joints that need loosening, and anyone seeking a truly stimulating way to stay healthy and strong during the winter months. Snowshoes are more user friendly than ever, and you don't need large tracts of wilderness to enjoy walking on snow, which allows first-timers to keep initial treks short and near civilization. Snowshoeing techniques can be learned and practiced in any undeveloped area with hardpack snow, from city parks to large backyards, before hitting a large forest where help is farther away and mistakes could prove more serious.

There are a number of tricks and techniques that can help beginners make the transition from earth to snow with as little clumsiness as possible. Hazards do exist, but even though most are easily avoided, too many novice snowshoers learn to recognize them the hard way. Following are what I consider the most useful tips for coping with different types of snow and terrain, and avoiding some of the most common snowshoeing dangers.

GETTING INTO SHAPE

Snowshoeing may be the most beneficial cardiovascular workout a human can get. Unlike jogging or running, there is virtually no impact on ankles or knees, and the activity itself can help reduce the possibility of coronary blockage to almost zero. The pace is slower than other winter sports, but beginners are often surprised to find that snowshoeing is much more tiring than they'd thought

Energy Expenditures for Snowshoeing and Comparable Activities*		
ACTIVITY/SPEED	TYPE OF TERRAIN	CALORIES/HOUR
Snowshoeing, 2.4 mph	Packed snow, flat trail	420
Snowshoeing, 3.0 mph	Packed snow, flat trail	510
Snowshoeing, 3.5 mph	Packed snow, flat trail	740
Snowshoeing, 3.3 mph	Powder snow, flat trail	744 (women)
		984 (men)
Snowshoeing, 2.9 mph	Powder snow, hilly trail	774 (women)
		1,046 (men)
Walking, 3.0 mph	Flat	335
Running, 5.2 mph	Flat	570
Running, 7.5 mph	Flat	890
Mountain biking	Rolling	550
XC skiing, 3.5 mph	Flat	600

* Studies courtesy Ball State University and the University of Vermont.

The author breaking trail in the Michigan woods. The relatively light clothing reflects the "hardening" effect of spending several days in the cold.

it would be. Or as one red-faced man of 25 told me after a half mile his first time out, "This is exhausting."

Ostensibly, an average human in an average day in civilization needs about 2,500 calories to remain healthy. Yet according to independent studies performed by Ball State University and the University of Vermont, an active snowshoer may burn a normal day's calories in under three hours, and can count on expending that much energy in under five hours.

The exertions of breaking trail notwithstanding, a snowshoer's metabolic rate also increases to compensate for exposure to cold—sort of like turning up the body's thermostat. Mountaineers call this autonomic adaptation to cold "hardening," and it's a process that everyone who spends a lot of time outside in winter will go through. After several days in a snow-locked wilderness it isn't unusual to see backpackers working ungloved and without a coat even in temperatures near zero.

Joints get a real workout when snowshoeing. The first complaint heard is nearly always about sharp pains in the hip joints, caused by a spread-footed walk, or straddle, wider than we're accustomed to. These sharp pains pass after two or three short outings, but be forewarned that snowshoeing, like any backwoods activity, requires strengthening a specific set of muscles and joints. I always keep the first snowshoeing trek of a winter short, about 2 miles or so, to work out any kinks in muscles and gear before I tackle the deep woods—where a failure in either could have unpleasant consequences.

In that same vein, be kind to yourself on the trail. Allow yourself plenty of time to complete any trek you've planned—I find that 2 miles per hour is a good rule of thumb. Don't resist the need to take breaks whenever you feel tired; there's nothing to be gained from beating your body into exhaustion—and maybe a good dose of hypothermia. Please consult your doctor prior to any outing if you have a history of hypertension or heart problems, even though snowshoeing may be just what the doctor ordered for many cardio-vascular maladies.

TRAILS

Probably most recreational snowshoers stick to established trails, where layers of snow compressed under their own weight and by previous traffic will in some places support a large man without snowshoes. Packed trails may still require snowshoes, especially when warmed by a midday sun, but comparatively little flotation is required to stay on top of them. For that reason, snowshoes made for trail use only are typically smaller than models designed for cross-country trekking and backpacking—8″×20″ is

Packed trails may still require snowshoes, especially when warmed by the midday sun.

typical. The smaller shoes are favorites with a growing number of people who run and race on established trails, but have too little flotation for any snow not already well packed or groomed.

Better for all-around hiking, in terms of weight, size, and load-bearing capacity are general-purpose shoes in the 9″×30″ category. This size is typically rated to support 250 pounds, and there is no snow a 9″×30″ 'shoe won't carry you over, even under a backpack. Flotation is more than adequate for light daypacking over unbroken trails, yet the size is small enough to negotiate overgrown swamps and frozen beaver floodings without becoming tangled in snow-locked brush.

Trail hiking is relatively free of terrain hazards, but be especially wary at stream crossings, springs, bridges, and narrow ledges, where light powder can conceal holes, undercuts, and hollows that are best not fallen into. A faceful of snow is usually funny to all parties, but having an undercut riverbank suddenly give way and send you sprawling into freezing water can be downright life threatening.

This particular lesson is fresh in my mind. Recently, while scouting for tracks along a local river, I had a porch-sized slab of hardened snow give way under me. I heard that distinctive thud-crunch-crack that precedes every cave-in, then a room-sized area under my feet tipped at a 30-degree angle and began sliding toward the rapids below. I dug the toe cleats of my snowshoes hard into the moving snow, dropped to a low crouch that enabled me to use my hands as support, and rode it out. The 2-ton slab shuddered and crunched to a halt against some large boulders several feet into the river, and I clambered back onto solid ground. Without the traction of crampon-type snowshoes I would almost certainly have rolled down that slippery slide and into the dark waters below.

Be aware, too, that a well-packed trail on a sunny day may in itself become a trail hazard. Snow compressed into a trail is more dense and melts more slowly than normal hardpack, so a warm day can turn well-used trails into slushy ridges whose edges may suddenly give way underfoot. Under such conditions, I generally find it more prudent to snowshoe alongside rather than directly on top of a trail. It means breaking a new trail, but the footing is more stable.

Be especially wary at stream crossings and ledges, where light powder can conceal undercuts.

If the trail is very hard underfoot, as well-used trails tend to become, you might find it more comfortable to remove your snowshoes and carry them. It might seem ironic, but a snowshoe that can carry its wearer across the deepest snows on earth is prohibitively clumsy on a solidly packed snowmobile trail.

Unfortunately, too many snowshoes are sold with no good way to carry them when they're off your feet. A 6-foot length of rope threaded through the binding holes of both shoes and tied together with a square knot forms a loop that can can be worn across the chest, under one arm, and over the opposite shoulder. This places the snowshoes across your back in a more or less convenient carry mode that leaves both hands free. Better than rope is a 6-foot utility strap with quick-release buckles, available at department stores for about $5.

POWDER

I believe fresh powder is the toughest snowshoeing medium, because the lead person is by definition breaking trail. Those who follow have it easier, but the trail breaker might have to lift each shoe an extra 4–6 inches to clear his own depressions. Breaking trail in powder is perhaps the best no-impact cardiovascular workout you can get; the trade-off is that it burns more energy per mile.

A typical general-purpose hiking snowshoe can handle any snow adequately, but untracked fluff is most easily broken with a larger model that provides more flotation, something in the 10"×36" range and rated to carry about 300 pounds. I believe the added weight of a larger 'shoe (about 4 ounces per 'shoe) is more than offset by not having to lift each one so high with every step. If you aren't alone, the chore of breaking trail can and should be

Breaking trail in fresh powder is perhaps the best no-impact cardiovascular activity you can get.

shared; when the lead person gets tired, he simply steps to one side and goes to the rear, leaving the next person in the lead. Everything being equal, this rotation technique permits a party of two to break trail twice as far as a lone snowshoer; a party of three, three times as far, and so on.

HARDPACK

Hardpack is the accumulation and subsequent concentration of several feet of snowfall into a thinner layer that has been compressed by the sun and by its own weight to a fraction of its original depth. Despite compression, hardpack layers can reach depths of more than 4 feet.

In temperatures below 20 degrees hardpack snow can approximate concrete in its hardness, and will sometimes support even an 800-pound elk. But let a weak winter sun soften that icy upper crust and each step can become a bone-jarring, crotch-deep fall. Warmed hardpack has far too much density to walk through, but not quite enough to walk atop. This means a hiker without snowshoes must push down hard with every step, breaking through the surface crust to whatever depth the snow underneath will support his weight. No one gets far in that kind of snow without snowshoes.

Because even softened hardpack is much denser than powder, a smaller and lighter snowshoe in the 9″×29″ range is nearly ideal for an average man. Women under 150 pounds can get by well enough on an even lighter shoe in the 8″×20″ range, though I wouldn't go smaller than that if you intend to leave a broken trail.

HILLS

Steep grades still pose a problem for most traditional-style wooden-frame snowshoes because they typically have inadequate traction and little holding power on grades, especially on loose powder. A good example of that occurred when biologists from the local Odawa tribe, wearing classic Michigan snowshoes, guided a tribal commissioner into an area where wolves had been hunting. When they reached a tall, steep ridge that had to be crossed, the commissioner, strapped into a pair of Tubbs's Altitudes, just grinned at his guides' snowshoes and said he'd wait for them at the top. The biologists climbed that wooded snowbound ridge literally on hands and knees while the commissioner made good on his boast and waited for them at its summit.

The Tubbs Quest 9"×29" showshoes with crampon (metal claw) bindings.

That incident illustrates how much improvement has gone into snowshoe traction in just recent years. If your snowshoes have crampon (metal claw) bindings with large turned-down serrated claws under the toes, most hills won't be much more than a good cardiovascular workout. Crampon-type bindings are designed to dig in at the toes, essentially hooking into the snow beneath to deliver very good braking and traction on both ascent and descent. Keep your weight on the balls of your feet when climbing up or down, and if the claws seem to slip a bit on loose powder, just press down harder until they dig in and hold.

A possible exception to the above might be the southeastern face of any tall wooded hill. Being leeward of the prevailing winds means that this side receives comparatively little snow, and what snow does accumulate is facing the sun. The result is often a thin layer of icy snow over concretelike earth that can resist the most aggressive crampons. Ascending and especially descending south-facing grades in that condition can be dangerous because crampons tend to skitter over frozen ground before stopping abruptly against a root or rock, which frequently sends a snowshoer into involuntary cartwheels.

If your shoes are the traditional wooden-frame type, many of which have only small steel ice claw hooks under the binding, hills require a bit more savvy to negotiate. South-facing hillsides receive more sun, so hardpack on them is often shallow enough to climb without snowshoes.

With traditional shoes, snowbound grades are best climbed by transversing, or climbing the slope diagonally. With this method the sides of your snowshoes provide traction by digging hard into the snow; you're making steps with the outside of the uphill shoe and the inside of the downhill shoe. Be aware that this method is a bit rough on snowshoe frames, so the lead snowshoer, who is cutting the steps, should wear the most stoutly built shoes.

Coming down hills can also be a challenge on wood-and-leather snowshoes because, again, most lack the traction to hold against a steep grade, something a traditional snowshoer should keep in mind always. My preferred technique in this case is to squat down onto the snowshoes until my buttocks are resting on top of their tails, and then sort of sled down the hill. Dragging gloved or mittened hands alongside will help you steer, and small trees work well for slowing or stopping if things begin moving too quickly. Snowshoeing and ski poles can be handy in this situation, though I generally just pick what looks like the easiest route and slide down like a kid on a toboggan.

An alternate, slightly more daring, method of descending steep hills on powder with conventional 'shoes is to essentially ski down them by placing one snowshoe ahead of the other and sliding to the bottom. This practice requires good balance and coordination, but it is a fun way to get downhill quickly. Be warned, however, that catching the toe of a 'shoe against a barely covered log or rock, or just having it nose-dive into the hardpack, can send you cartwheeling downhill. Try to keep your weight back on your heels, and never attempt to use this sliding method on any grade you wouldn't want to tumble down.

ICE

Often, cutting across a frozen pond or lake is the shortest and flattest distance between two points, but I cannot overstress the importance of using caution when snowshoeing over any body of frozen water. A deep-frozen beaver pond in January might be covered by as much as 3 feet of ice, enough to support a truckload of fishermen. But that same ice might be only a couple of inches thick in certain areas, so every snowshoer should know how to "read" ice

Snowshoes can be a lifesaver if you're caught without them and need to slog through heavy snow to reach civilization. While any of the commercially-made 'shoes described in this book would be better to use, if you have to do it yourself, here's how:

You will need a sturdy butt knife and eight or ten more or less straight lengths of green wood at least an inch in diameter (four or five pieces per shoe). The frame of the shoe is essentially an elongated triangle, with the base formed by a foot-long crosspiece lashed across the ends of two 3-foot lengths. The heel, or pointed end of the frame, is made by lashing the free ends of the longer pieces together. Whittle notches halfway through each piece where it joins with another to help lock the component lengths more tightly when they're lashed in place.

The last and most critical part of an emergency snowshoe is the arch crosspiece (or crosspieces, as in the illustration), the piece your foot will be on while walking. It must be positioned to span the longer lengths of the frame at a point where the tail (pointed) end is heaviest and swivels downward when the shoe is raised, but far enough from the front crosspiece to allow clearance between itself and your boot toes. It's important that the tail of each shoe drags, or "tracks," when you raise your foot to take a step, because tracking helps keep the shoe from twisting underfoot while raising the front upward to avoid tripping hazards. When you've determined the best location for the arch crosspiece(s), notch the intersections and lash them tightly together.

The final step is to fasten the snowshoes to your feet and walk home. With your boot heel pressed against the arch crosspiece(s), lay the center of a 2-foot length of cord across your instep, wrap the ends under the crosspiece(s), then cross the ends over your instep, around the ankle, and tie them as you would a shoe. There may be a tendency for the snowshoes to slip sideways while walking, and if this becomes a problem you can fix it by cutting shallow grooves in the arch crosspiece(s) on each side of your boots to help anchor the binding cord.

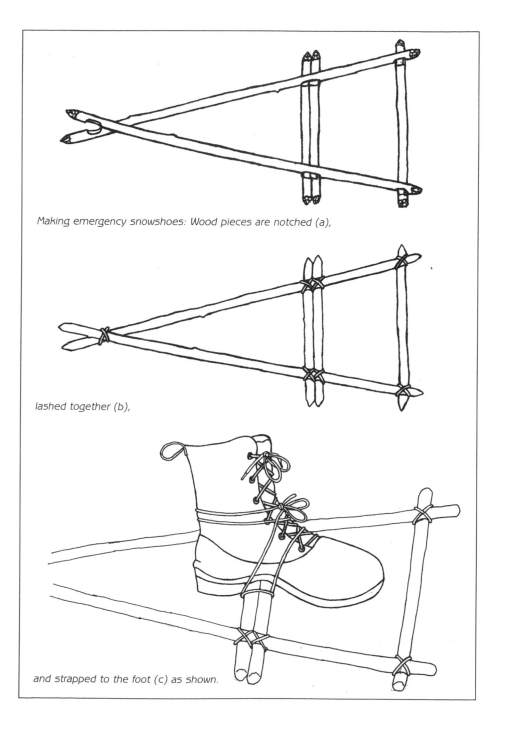

Making emergency snowshoes: Wood pieces are notched (a),

lashed together (b),

and strapped to the foot (c) as shown.

and identify common hazards that should be avoided on any frozen body of water.

First, always bear in mind that a whole-body dunking can kill you quickly, and will incapacitate the strongest man almost immediately. If you fall through ice over 6 feet of water, or headlong into a shallow river, the least you can look forward to is an immediate and completely debilitating case of severe hypothermia. Within seconds after climbing or being pulled from the water a soaked dunking victim will involuntarily curl into a fetal position, shivering so violently it hurts, and with almost no control over physical functions. Almost no one will have the ability or time to save themselves, and without immediate treatment (see chapter 5) a dunking in subfreezing weather is likely to be fatal.

The aforementioned beaver pond is bound to be fed by, and to empty into, a flowing stream. The same goes for many inland lakes, which are often interconnected by a chain of streams. Both the inlets and outlets of those streams will be marked by thin ice, kept that way by the friction of constantly moving water beneath. Never approach open water, and always stay at least 10 feet away from dead trees sticking up from beaver floodings; the ice around these trunks is kept weak by water lapping against them from below.

Thin ice can often be identified by a dark color. The thinner the ice, the more visible will be the dark waters underneath, so the darker the ice, the thinner it's likely to be. Before crossing any pond or lake (I try never to snowshoe across rivers) I like to chop a hole through the ice near shore with my always present survival knife. If I have to hack through 4 inches before hitting water, I figure it's safe to snowshoe across. But expect that stream inlets and outlets will be mostly concealed, especially after a fresh snowfall, and steer well clear of the telltale furrow of any stream at water's edge.

More insidious are flowing springs. Many are actually small underground creeks, covered over by centuries of fallen logs and debris. These are typically found along shorelines, where water is usually no more than knee deep. Again, avoid any dark ice you see, and expect that ice along any shoreline might be kept treacherously thin by lapping water.

As any ice fisherman who's ever slammed his buttocks against a hard-frozen surface knows well, ice itself can be a danger. A warm sun or unseasonable rain can melt hardpack lying atop the ice, first turning it to slush, then freezing it to a hard and extremely slippery surface. Resist the temptation to remove your snowshoes on ice, because not only do they increase the amount of area over which your weight is distributed, but their cleats provide sure footing on the slipperiest ice.

Despite those avoidable hazards, a hard-frozen lake offers some of the best snowshoeing to be found anywhere. There are no hills, no ravines, and no tangles of undergrowth to push through. A good many animals, from otters and coyotes to wolves and deer, appreciate the easy travel afforded by frozen waters, making such places a good bet for wildlife photographers.

Frozen lakes are often very cold because their large flat surfaces channel winds, often in a different direction than prevailing air currents and sometimes with considerable force. Snowshoers who venture across any large expanse of ice should expect subzero wind-chills, stinging wind-driven snow, and a real potential for frostbite on exposed skin. A hooded windproof parka shell and gloves are the uniform of the day, with a ski mask or wool scarf held in reserve for those places where the wind is strong and cold enough to literally take your breath away. Snowshoeing across a frozen lake is actually an exhilarating experience, but you must be dressed for the conditions or it can be miserable.

FIELD REPAIRS

While almost unheard of today, it's still possible to break a snowshoe frame by bridging it across two solid points. Depending on snow conditions and the distance you have to travel, a broken snowshoe frame can be a real inconvenience—or maybe even life threatening.

A roll of duct tape is an essential part of any snowshoe field repair kit. The tough, sticky stuff adheres well even to wet surfaces, and a couple of dozen wraps can by themselves hold a broken snowshoe frame together for several miles. Broken decking can be expediently replaced by wrapping several turns of duct tape around the entire snowshoe frame over the damaged area.

More properly, the snowshoe frame should be splinted, much like a broken limb. This is done by taping four stout sticks across the break, one on top, one on the bottom, and one on each side. The splints need not be fancy, but should be at least 6 inches long to completely and securely span the break. Each splint should be taped in place independently of the others at both ends before wrapping them all together in a cocoon of duct tape.

The best frame splint I've found for tubular-frame models is a short piece of PVC plastic pipe with an inside diameter of 1 inch, or large enough to slide over your snowshoe's frame without being loose enough to be sloppy. Slip the section of PVC over both ends of the separated frame, positioning it so that it spans both sides of the separation in its center, then securely tape both ends of the pipe section to the frame with several turns of duct tape. It isn't a permanent fix, but any of these snowshoe splints will allow a broken 'shoe to function well enough to get you out of the woods.

I also recommend having at least 6 feet of stout but flexible rope (heavy clothesline, parachute cord) to repair or replace broken bindings. As mentioned elsewhere, a snowshoe binding simply se-

cures the snowshoe to its wearer's foot. There are dozens of proprietary methods for doing that, but I've yet to find a model that
couldn't also be fastened securely enough with a length of rope.

SNOWSHOE MAINTENANCE

Snowshoes are not high maintenance, and as my made-in-
1945 bearpaws demonstrate, a little care can help ensure that yours
will deliver years of reliable service. Traditional wood-and-leather
snowshoes suffer from the decay and wear common to both these
natural materials. A thick, usually rubberized, coat of lacquer
polyurethane applied at the factory will resist abrasion and water
damage for up to several seasons, but at some point both snowshoes will need retreating. When your 'shoes will reach that point is
subject to the amount of use they've seen, but dull-colored wood or
leather webbing that turns white after drying is a sure sign that a
recoating is needed.

Probably the easiest way to protect your traditional 'shoes
from dry rot is to simply send them back to their maker and have
it done professionally using tanks, chemicals, and heating equipment that most snowshoers don't have. An added benefit is that the
craftsmen who made your snowshoes will know them and their
bindings better than a snowshoe rental and repair shop. Shipping a
pair of snowshoes via UPS costs about $8, with a good recoating
running around $25.

If factory recoating isn't possible, a good rubberized marine
varnish, about $10 a pint at most hardware stores, will suffice to
protect frames and webbing. It won't wear as well or as long as factory finishes, and you'll probably be griped at when you do send
them back to the maker, but off-the-shelf coatings will work well
enough when there's nothing else.

Although more impervious to the elements than traditional 'shoes, modern synthetic models also require a little TLC to maximize their life and minimize the possibility of failure. Deckings made of neoprene, Hypalon™, ArcTec™, or rubberized nylon are not harmed by moisture, but they should be stored in a shaded place where the sun's UV rays can't deteriorate and possibly crack the fabric. Silicone-based treatments like Armor-All®, offer good protection from premature aging, but remember that such stuff is also extremely slippery, and apply it with discretion.

Stainless-steel and aluminum decking rivets, frames, crampon claws, and hinge pins will oxidize or rust if stored untreated over a summer. My favorite long-term storage treatment for these parts is a light coat of ordinary cooking oil. After several hours the oil will congeal into a gummy, waterproof skin that protects against corrosion, but doesn't require removal before the snowshoe is used.

The most important snowshoe maintenance tip is also the easiest, and that is simply to keep your snowshoes dry whenever they're not on your feet. This especially applies to snowshoes with zip-shut carrying bags. Synthetic or not, storing wet snowshoes in a warm enclosed place will induce mold and mildew to rot decking, prompt stainless steel to rust, and corrode aluminum frames. If you can't properly dry your 'shoes at the end of an outing, try to keep them frozen outside the door or in the trunk of a car, because decay all but ceases below the freezing point.

4

Snowshoeing Activities

Whenever nonsnowshoers tell me that walking on snow sounds like a boring winter pastime to them, I have to chuckle. The truth is that snowshoeing can be as much excitement as most of us would ever want, even dangerous to the foolhardy; it just depends on the activity and circumstances encountered. Being far from civilization during a blizzard that closes down an entire state's highways is probably the most isolation you can find on planet earth, and it's an experience I can recommend to everyone.

But you must go prepared, because cold victimizes only those who haven't guarded themselves against it. How challenging or serene a snowshoe outing turns out depends in large amount on how much forethought was put into the trip, and even then nature may test the experts' survival skills from time to time. It doesn't pay to underestimate nature or to overestimate yourself in snow country. Lessons learned there the hard way are generally painful and are probably best learned by vicarious means.

Following is a summary of the most popular snowshoeing activities, with tips and advice for getting the most enjoyment from each. Not one of them is boring, and every one beats spending Sunday afternoon in an armchair-induced trance.

DAYHIKING

Dayhiking is the most popular snowshoeing activity among beginners and veterans alike because, as the name implies, it doesn't require more than a few hours of free time and a good snow base. Small city and roadside parks will suffice, so beginners needn't get

Dayhiking requires only a few hours of free time and a good snow base.

far from civilization, and even the most addicted workaholic can find time and space for a stroll on snowshoes. In fact, a few busy executive types I know have found that an hour or two of snowshoeing clears the mind and allows creative juices to flow.

Since dayhikers aren't planning to spend the night, they don't need to hump a sleeping bag, tent, stove, and most of the other weight that backpackers require. Carrying less weight means you can get by on a smaller, lighter snowshoe because you won't need so much flotation.

If the objective is simply to get exercise on a packed and well-marked hiking or snowmobile trail, a snowshoe like Atlas's 8"×25" Hiking Series (up to 200 pounds) is suitable for an average snowshoer. Again, I prefer the increased flotation of at least a 9"×29" snowshoe because I can never resist leaving a beaten path to investigate some point of interest. A working-sized snowshoe is a little heavier on the trail, but provides the flotation necessary to cut cross-country over any type of snow or terrain should the need (or just the desire) arise.

Being lightly equipped doesn't mean going unprepared. Even short hikes away from civilization (that is, immediate medical and other help) should never be undertaken without loading a day- or fanny pack with necessities. Those essentials should include the Basic Three—map and compass, fire-starting kit, and survival knife—followed by a canteen, first-aid kit, high-carbohydrate snacks to stoke the metabolic furnace, dry socks, and so on. A daypack also allows convenient carry of garment layers too warm to wear on the trail; much more comfortable than tying your jacket around your waist.

One item that I very much recommend all snowshoers have at all times is a good flashlight. Only recently I was guiding Odawa biologists who actually seemed surprised when darkness settled over the forest at 5 P.M. Our only means of keeping to the vague and unbroken trail that led out of that darkened cedar swamp was by following blue spray-painted blaze marks on tree trunks with the beam of my flashlight. Neither of my companions had thought to bring a flashlight, but none of us could see without it.

To date the only flashlights I've deemed reliable enough to carry in the woods are made by the Mag Instrument Company, better known for the brand name Mag-Lite. I generally have three: a two-AA Mini-Mag ($12) in a holster on my hip, a one-AAA Solitaire ($8) tied to my survival knife sheath, and another Solitaire on my key ring. All have bright, focusable beams, rugged aluminum bodies, waterproof construction, and a spare bulb in their tailcaps. Under normal use, I change the alkalines in my Mini-Mag about every two months; about every six months for the less used Solitaires.

For daypacking I've grown fond of Mag's two-D-cell model ($20)—the larger, heavier, and brighter three- and four-D-cell models I generally only carry on my equipment saucer. Like other Mag-Lites, these models carry a spare bulb in their tailcaps and deliver dependable light for up to a year of normal use before requiring fresh batteries. All have brilliant, focusable beams that go from spotlight to floodlight by twisting the head, and all have push-button switches that can be used to send flash signals at night.

FASTPACKING

When it takes all day to reach that special ice-fishing hole or remote campsite, and all the time you can spare is a weekend, the faster the trek to and from, the more time you'll have to enjoy doing what you came for. This is the domain of fastpacking, or ultralight backpacking for those seeking less time on the trail than at their destinations.

If you're an adventurer, fastpacking is a great way to see a lot of country in a short time. The sport has been growing among young folks, who view getting from one point to another in the shortest time as something of a challenge. Most will also tell you there's a truly spiritual aspect to snowshoeing an expanse of wilderness so large that it cannot be crossed on foot in a single day.

Like daypackers, fastpackers want as light a snowshoe (and everything else) as they can use. Unlike daypackers, winter fastpackers are carrying 30 to 40 pounds of necessities all day long through sometimes rugged and untracked wilderness.

Deadfalls, never-frozen springheads, and Olympic-sized hills are to be anticipated whenever your route leaves established trails, and sometimes even when it doesn't. Such activity demands the flotation of a working-sized (9″×29″ or larger) shoe rated for at least 250 pounds, regardless of how little you and your gear actually weigh. I usually opt for a larger trail-breaker 'shoe in the 10″×36″ category (300-plus pounds), even though they are more difficult to manipulate in thick undergrowth.

Fastpacking is essentially daypacking, except that spending a night or two requires the additional weight and bulk of a warm bedroll, shelter, and food. For fastpackers the number of items considered necessary is dictated primarily by the amount of weight an individual can carry comfortably for hours at a stretch. "Luxuries" like a comprehensive first-aid kit, spare compass, radio receiver, extra long johns, and diverse menu are sacrificed to save weight, space, calories, and time.

A sleeping pad is an absolute must when lying prone on the world's best heat sink. As a boy I had to make my own sleeping pallets from branches and pine boughs, but while these were much preferred to having my body heat sucked into the earth, they were invariably bumpy and uncomfortable to sleep on.

Today a good nonbumpy, closed-cell sleeping pad will cost

from $12 for Slumberjack's R3 to $25 for the folding Z-Rest from Cascade Designs. Unlike heavier and less compactible inflatable pads, which I never recommend for backpacking, closed-cell foam is unharmed by punctures and tears, impervious to water, and provides an effective barrier against cold.

Probably most weight-conscious fastpackers carry a sleeping bag in the 20-degree range, even though nighttime temperatures might actually fall below zero. To compensate, they use numerous little tricks to boost the bag's efficiency on subzero nights. Like sliding an emptied backpack or zipped-up parka shell over the foot of the bag to provide an extra layer of insulating air in that critical area. Or sleeping with a tightly capped canteen of warmed water as a hot-water bottle, which also ensures a supply of unfrozen water for coffee in the morning. On very cold nights I've often covered my entire body with a light tarpaulin or groundsheet, which adds another 10 degrees of protection.

Shelter is most often an ultralight tube-type bivy—not recommended for the claustrophobic. These average about 2 pounds in their stuff sacks, and despite being a little tight they offer unheard-of portable protection from the elements. With no space for stove and mess kit, meals are simply unwrapped and eaten, and there's little room for extras.

Carrying fewer amenities also means there is less latitude for mistakes in an environment that tends to punish the unwary, so fastpacking should be attempted only by experienced winter campers. Even then, caution and forethought are the order of each day. Never fastpack alone, and always let someone in civilization know your route and estimated timetable. Few fastpacking trips are anything but terrific experiences, but it's comforting to know that someone will know when to expect you and where to come looking should you be waylaid by circumstance.

BACKPACKING

Backpackers have it all covered, which explains why I haven't been dead in the woods during snowstorms that local authorities thought had killed me. A properly outfitted backpack will keep its owner living comfortably, regardless of weather or temperature, at least until its food runs out. Even then it will continue to provide shelter, warmth, and all the other necessities of survival for an indefinite period. The forces of fate notwithstanding, a modern backpacker with even mediocre equipment and training is all but impervious to weather and environmental hazards that have killed many a professional woodsman in generations past. Personally, I get a little rush out of being completely cut off from civilization by a winter storm that paralyzes entire states for days at a time.

The trade-off is that being prepared for everything means hauling a lot of gear, and that of course means more weight. Probably most fully equipped backpackers travel only 3–5 miles before making camp in a place where they might stay for the duration, dayhiking from there each day.

Improvements in materials and manufacturing methods have reduced the weight of my winter bedroll alone from 12 to 4 pounds since my first winter campout, but so too have those technologies resulted in more gear. While some engineers strove to reduce the weight of existing gear, many more were designing water filters, fire starters, and ultralight sleeping pads that are today deemed essential. It seems that wherever I shave off a pound, I wind up adding as much in the form of some useful tool or device that hadn't been available or possible just a few years ago. Because of that, my own winter backpacking load seems to be stuck between 60 and 65 pounds, the prescribed one-third of my body weight.

Humping a heavy pack over snow of any depth is much tougher than carrying the same load in summer, especially over unbroken trail. Because of that, one item I've long considered crucial to backpacking or otherwise hauling a lot of weight on snowshoes is a plastic snow saucer, like those used by kids for sliding down hills. I've used a saucer for hauling gear since I was a boy, because it's much easier to tow a heavy load over snow than to carry it.

Winter camp. My snow saucer is at left.

These toys retail for under $10, yet convert simply and inexpensively to a serious snow-trekking tool capable of hauling loads of more than 40 pounds with ease.

To convert a sliding saucer to snowshoeing use, first drill 0.5-inch-diameter holes spaced about 6 inches apart around the saucer's perimeter. I generally use a survival knife for that task, but an electric drill or old soldering iron works equally well. These holes are for tying off ungainly items, and have never weakened the structural integrity of any saucers I've used. Eight feet of cord tied through two of those holes at what will be the front provides the means to tow the loaded saucer.

Next I tie off a plastic-fiber 100-pound feed sack, available for about $2 at most feed stores, by its bottom corners through two holes at the rear of the saucer. With the sack filled and tied shut, then anchored with cord to holes in the saucer's perimeter, you have a virtually indestructible sled that tows a maximum of gear with a minimum of effort. The saucer's rounded bottom helps reduce friction between itself and the snow, and its circular shape lets it slide around obstacles. Occasionally my saucer will flip upside down while being hauled over deadfallen logs, but a quick flick of the towropes rights it again, and if the load is secured well, no harm is done.

Beaver trappers in my home range often use plastic boats, just like or similar to the kind kids use for snow sliding. A boat's deep bathtub shape can haul far more gear than a saucer, and a common mistake is filling up the sled with more weight than its owner can comfortably tow. Because of their squarish corners, boats tend to snag and capsize against obstacles that a saucer would slide over or around. For transporting heavy loads on packed trails, a boat is a good choice, but if you intend to be breaking trail through bobcat country, I'd recommend the saucer.

While a snow saucer or boat can greatly increase the number

of amenities a snowshoer can take into the woods, I must warn against hauling all the proverbial eggs in that single basket. Keep vital items like sleeping bag and tent on your back, because I've seen for myself that it isn't impossible for a gear saucer to go sliding away into a river or crevice for no good reason.

OBSERVING WILDLIFE

If ever there was a good reason to be a snowshoer, it has to be the wildlife activity you see almost everywhere. Winter is a lean time for deer, elk, moose, and most other nonhibernators, and those animals are forced to be more active when snow covers their summertime food plants. Of course, that also applies to the predators that regard those herbivores as food. Few memories are as treasured by me as the 100-yard staring match I once held with a gray wolf, or the sight of river otters repeatedly catching and eating small panfish on a frozen beaver pond.

There are several reasons why snowshoers are more likely to see wild animals than are other winter enthusiasts. Snowmobiles generate noise, stench, light, and motion—virtually everything that might alert wildlife to their approach. Cross-country skiers seldom try to break trail through swamp, and those who make the attempt once never try it twice. Both those modes of transport rely heavily on established trails that tend to be shunned by wild animals precisely because they are established trails.

But while deep snows impede the travel of most other humans and animals alike, a snowshoer can walk almost anywhere at will. I've often taken animals by surprise in places where they never expected to see a person, and winter is the only season in which almost anyone can track down a wild animal. It's easy to see how

Native Americans armed with spears and stone-tipped arrows would have found large animals to be easier prey in winter.

The same goes for a modern snowshoer armed with a camera, and anyone who ventures into the woods without one will probably regret that decision. A snow-locked forest looks, smells, and feels clean; not barren at all, but whittled down to just the strongest and most capable survivors. Preoccupied by a hunger to acquire the calories needed to maintain body heat, many animals fail to notice the quiet approach of a human on snowshoes, so photo opportunities are usually frequent.

Cold can be hard on cameras. Shutters can operate at reduced speeds or not at all, ice can collect on lenses, and optics fog. Sub-zero temperatures can make film brittle, and the tiny epoxy-bedded microchips in programmable cameras could crack (the same applies to anything else electronic). I selected both the 35mm cameras I use professionally, a Pentax K1000 and a Ricoh KR-5, because they operate manually.

Lenses do not fog with condensation when taken from warm to cold, but taking any optical instrument from cold to warm will result in a heavy collection of moisture on the outer lens surfaces. That means the best place for your camera is outside your clothing, constantly exposed to cold air. A small air-activated toe-warmer packet rubber-banded to the back of a camera provides enough warmth to keep electronics from freezing, but usually not enough to cause fogging on lenses.

You'll also want a good binocular, because while all wild species are quick to detect motion at more than 100 yards, many cannot make out a stationary human form past 50 yards. A binocular enhances our innate optical advantage over most forest dwellers, permitting a quiet snowshoer who approaches from downwind to clearly observe animals without being detected by them.

My favorite binocular is Leupold's 10×28 Gold Ring roof prism model—and with a retail price of $650 it had better be my favorite. However, you can get by very well with Tasco's 8×21 mini binocular, also a roof prism model, with nicely coated optics, rubber armor, and a price tag that averages under $40. There are dozens of binocular makes and models in almost every price range, but binos are one item that can usually be tried out before purchasing, so shop around for the one that best suits your eyes and your budget.

Snowshoers seeking to photograph or observe wildlife can make good use of military surplus white winter camouflage shells. There are lots of camouflage patterns made to match various types of terrain, but none is more effective than plain old white against a snowy background. I've approached browsing deer to within 30 feet while 'shoeing in my "winter whites," and that's about as close as a person is likely to get to being undetectable by wildlife.

Price for the cotton shell military trousers and hooded jacket outfit is a rather steep $50, but there are less expensive means of becoming hard to see on snow. Oversized white sweatpants, sized large enough to slide over your trousers, are an effective substitute for around $10, though you'll probably need to cut the elastic around each ankle cuff to slide them over your pac boots. An equally oversized white hooded sweatshirt, about $15, worn over your parka shell completes the outfit. I've even cut a hole through the center of an old white bedsheet and worn it as a poncho.

Each of the aforementioned garments is made all or mostly from cotton, and all can absorb their own weight in water. This is not a desirable quality for any item of cold-weather clothing, but presents no real danger in this case alone. Because it is worn over a stand-alone cold-weather outfit, very little body heat escapes to the camo shell. Kept below freezing, the cotton fabric neither melts nor absorbs snow. If it does get wet, those spots will simply freeze without affecting the integrity or warmth of the clothing beneath.

KNOWING YOUR LIMITS

First-time snowshoers often describe the activity as exhausting, and even veteran snow walkers consider a short 5-mile outing to be an exhilarating lung stretcher. A typical snowshoer burns an average of 800 calories for every hour on the trail—often less, but frequently much more. Because snowshoeing is a casual impact-free sport that takes place in a distractingly beautiful environment, beginning 'shoers are sometimes surprised by energy expenditures that may consume triple the calories they're accustomed to burning. Hypoglycemia, a sudden drop in available blood sugars that sometimes causes victims to feel fatigued or dizzy, or even to lose conciousness, is discussed in chapter 5.

Don't overdo it. For neophytes and veterans alike, the first outing of every winter should be an easy jaunt, not too far from house or car. Give yourself and your muscles a few miles to become accustomed to the unique physical demands of walking on hardpack, because a charley-horse cramp can take a whole lot of the fun out of any outing. Worse, trying to push on with fatigued muscles not yet adapted to walking on snow results in an increasing loss of balance and coordination, and that can lead to a regrettable slip or misstep. Be kind to yourself and have fun.

Cold-Weather Hazards

Snowshoeing is a much safer activity than fast-moving winter sports like snowboarding or downhill skiing, and it's infinitely safer than riding today's overpowered snowmobiles. But the potential for being injured while snowshoeing does exist, however slight, and many of those injuries are likely to be caused or exacerbated by cold. Avoidance and prevention might not always be adequate protection from the fickle winds of fate, so a savvy snowshoer should know what to expect and stand ready to treat most common cold-related injuries.

HYPOTHERMIA

Hypothermia is a potentially serious loss of body heat that can occur in temperatures as high as 60 degrees, and it represents the most common hazard faced by campers the world over in any season. If a cold spring evening in Florida can induce fatal hypothermia in just hours, as it did when three U.S. Army Rangers died while training in the Everglades in 1993, the potential faced by snowshoers needs no further explanation.

The first stage of hypothermia is uncontrollable shivering. At this point it becomes a priority to immediately rewarm the victim's body. A warm (never hotter than body temperature) shower or bath is ideal, but a campfire has sufficed many times. Remove and replace the victim's wet clothing with dry garments if that is possible, and get him to drink warm liquids. Gently rubbing the limbs can help get circulation and warmth flowing better in the initial stages of hypothermia, but be gentle with tissue that might already be cold-damaged.

A cure for mild hypothermia that has worked well for me is to tape, tie, or belt an air-activated chemical handwarmer packet over each of the victim's kidneys, on top of his clothing but beneath his jacket. (Kidneys are located in the lumbar region of the back, just above either hip.) All blood in the body passes through the kidneys once about every four minutes, so applying a source of heat over those organs is effective for rewarming victims at any stage of hypothermia. Just be sure not to apply direct heat greater than body temperature to bare skin, even if it feels good to the victim, because the already weakened skin might burn and blister.

If none of this is possible, force the victim to walk at as quick a pace as possible. He probably won't feel like exercise, but force the issue anyway, even to the point of making him fighting mad. Anger induces adrenaline flow, and mountain climbers pack syrettes of this hormone because it remains perhaps the most effective emergency treatment for hypothermia.

If loss of body heat continues, the victim will experience crippling abdominal cramps, delusional babbling, and then unconciousness. When his internal organs cool to 85 degrees, death is near and only a hospital is likely to save his life. Even with prompt medical treatment a victim whose internal temperature has reached 83 degrees has only a one in three chance of survival. At an internal temperature of 70 degrees life will probably cease entirely.

An often repeated bit of advice is to never eat snow because it brings down your body temperature. That's true, and people have actually died from hypothermia induced by eating snow. But I frequently eat snow when I'm backpacking because it cools me during times of heavy perspiration. If you're feeling overheated, eating snow can help, but never eat snow if you're feeling chilled.

FROSTBITE

Anyone who has seen a frozen vegetable or hot dog has seen frostbite, flesh in which all moisture has frozen into ice crystals. Animals that hibernate never freeze, not even frogs and turtles that winter under the muddy bottoms of ponds, because no animal can survive having the water in its tissues frozen solid.

The first level of frostbite is sometimes called "frostnip" because the affliction hasn't yet fully sunk its icy teeth. Exposed skin, especially that over fingers and knuckles, turns white from lack of blood circulation and from the formation of ice crystals in the upper epidermal layers. At this point a victim has already sustained tissue damage similar to a second-degree burn.

Next is a slow, painful freezing of fat, muscle, and eventually bone. This is true frostbite, because the effect is death to at least part of an affected limb. At that stage amputation of the dead areas becomes necessary to head off gangrene and the systemic infection it creates.

As with all physical calamaties, the first step in dealing with frostbite is to avoid it altogether. Be aware that the thinner, less insulated skin on your hands, cheekbones, nose, and chin will be most susceptible to injury from exposure to cold. If you feel a tingling of cold in any of these areas, immediately cover the area with gloves, scarf, or hat, and rewarm the tissues as soon as possible. Never attempt to rub circulation back into frostbitten tissues, as doing so guarantees you'll destroy many frozen but otherwise intact blood vessels.

WARMING COLD FEET AND HANDS

Cold hands and feet can be effectively warmed by using the Inuit trick of placing them directly against the bare belly of a companion, but this treatment must never be attempted by anyone who feels cold himself. Better yet is to apply a cloth-wrapped hand-warmer packet onto the affected area, but never apply heat greater than body temperature directly or you might damage the skin further. A pan or bucket of lukewarm water is the most effective treatment for frostbite, if one is available, but the rewarming process should begin immediately with whatever is available.

DEHYDRATION

Dehydration is a real hazard in the winter woods because snowshoers burn more than twice the calories expended by an average person in civilization, and that means perspiration. But loss of body moisture isn't always obvious in winter because good insulating materials wick it away to evaporate, leaving their wearer feeling dry and warm rather than hot and sweaty.

Symptoms of dehydration include feeling cold, because like an automobile, your body uses water for both heating and cooling.

Urine becomes less diluted and darker in color—a warning that toxins are not being flushed adequately from the kidneys—and mild to severe constipation will probably result.

Preventing and curing dehydration is as simple as drinking liquids until fluid levels return to normal, evidenced by clear urine and easy bowel movements. Water is probably best, but any soup or beverage will work to replace lost liquids. Conventional wisdom warns against drinks like coffee, tea, and hot cocoa because caffeine is diuretic, meaning that it prompts your kidneys to expel more than they take in. In real life the point is moot, because if you're drinking enough of any beverage you'll stay well hydrated.

SNOW BLINDNESS

Snow is a more brilliant surface than many snowshoers have realized until it was too late. As outdoor photographers know, sunlit snow makes any setting many times brighter than the same place without snow. That increased intensity can make sensitive optical instruments malfunction, or even cause them damage.

That goes especially for human eyes. Snow blindness is a debilitating, though usually temporary, shutdown of the eyes caused by overloading the optical nerves with too much light—sort of like sunburn of the eyeballs. Except in this instance the affected organs turn themselves off to avoid further damage. The resulting blindness isn't usually serious in itself, but the dangers posed by losing your sight for a day or more in a winter woods are obvious.

Snow blindness doesn't happen suddenly, and there are usually plenty of warning signs before your optical nerves stop functioning. Usually first is a sharp headache, caused by involuntarily squinting your eyes against the glare, and sometimes accompanied by bright spots. Next comes scratchy, sometimes itchy eyeballs that feel dry in their sockets. Conversely, some folks have also experienced uncontrolled watering of their eyes.

If you experience any of these symptoms, immediately shield your eyes from sunlight by whatever means are available. The old survivalist trick of wearing a slitted mask of birch bark tied around the head is still a good last-ditch remedy. But sunglasses, a tube of mosquito netting, or a brimmed hat worn low are all more effective, and a lot more comfortable to wear.

In a case of full-blown snow blindness, a victim will be able to see little or not at all. Wrap the eyes to seal out all light and get the victim to a doctor as quickly as possible. If for some reason medical attention is unavailable, keep the victim's eyes bandaged against light for at least three days. If he cannot see by that time, rewrap his eyes and wait two more days before again exposing them to light.

HYPOGLYCEMIA

Hypoglycemia is a medical term for low blood-sugar levels, and it's an affliction that every snowshoer can expect to face. Modern humans are accustomed to being extraordinarily well fed, not used to drawing from their bodies' fat reserves when readily available energy in the form of blood sugars is depleted.

Snowshoeing burns bloodborne calories about three times as quickly as most of us are accustomed to, so energy levels are expended more quickly. When blood sugars fall below normal levels, prompting a body to begin drawing from its fat reserves, the brain often perceives that as a starvation threat and begins shutting down bodily systems to conserve energy. The results, as my teenage nephew discovered when he blacked out momentarily and sat in a campfire (he was unhurt, thank God), can range from overwhelming fatigue to outright loss of consciousness.

PARASITES

Subfreezing weather does not kill waterborne parasites like *Giardia, Cryptosporidium,* and *Cyclospora,* or many insects and spiders for that matter. Spiders can often be seen atop the snow when a warm sun fools them into thinking it's spring, and parasites ingested from an icy spring will react likewise to their new host's body heat. Drinking water drawn from any natural source except clean melted snow must be treated to either remove parasites or kill them.

Removal of parasitic organisms and harmful bacteria is the preferred method of water purification for most folks, and that requires a water filter unit. I've been packing one of these handy little safety items since 1997, when we were informed—after a friend learned the hard way—that iodine does not kill *Cryptosporidium* or the newly discovered *Cyclospora* flagellates.

A concern about using water filters in winter is that they might freeze. Because I've had no choice, I've used my SweetWater Guardian+Plus, MSR WaterWorks II, PUR Voyageur and Scout, and neat Seychelle Bottoms-Up squeeze bottle filters in temperatures down to −10 degrees. I do make certain that filter chambers and hoses are purged after each use, but none has failed to function on those subzero mornings when I've used them to draw coffee water from icy flowing springs and rivers.

Heating water to a boil kills everything in it, and boiling remains the best sterilization method available today. Boiling doesn't remove amoebae, bacteria, or viruses, but it does render all of them harmless (dead), and there are certain mineral-rich streams I prefer to drink without filtering.

Some confusion exists about long water must be boiled before it's safe for consumption. The truth is that nearly all harmful organisms are killed at 180 degrees, while water boils at 212 degrees at sea level. A rolling boil is simply a visual verification that the water is safe to drink, a much less painful method than sticking your finger into the pot. High-country snowshoers who get above 3,000 feet, where the air gets thin and atmospheric pressure decreases, should cover their pots with a loose lid to increase the pressure and heat inside.

Never put hot water into a canteen or water bottle unless you intend to sleep with it next to your body—a handy winter camping foot warmer and remedy for hypothermia. Hot water actually freezes faster than cold water, a phenomenon that has taken many snowshoers by surprise.

Never fill any canteen or water bottle to its top in freezing air temperatures. Moving water doesn't freeze nearly as quickly as still water, so leaving a canteen only half full so the water inside sloshes around will help keep it from freezing. In camp, canteens and water bottles should be left empty until needed.

The Odawa biologists I track for must have unfrozen water to make plaster casts of tracks even in subzero weather. Their neat little solution is to slip an activated handwarmer packet into their canteen case, or to duct-tape it to a water bottle. This trick also works well to keep drinking water, sport drinks, and other beverages available for consumption on the trail.

AVALANCHES

Snowslides, called avalanches in mountain areas, are more common than many realize—an assertion supported by the number of folks who have been buried by them. Injurious and sometimes fatal snowslides have occurred from New York to Idaho, and none of the victims understood the danger they faced until a wave of fast-moving snow had engulfed them.

One common misconception about snowslides is that victims are simply washed under by a wall of soft, fluffy snow. The truth is that several tons of snow slipping downhill as fast as gravity and friction allow is sure to bring with it boulders of ice, large rocks, and even tree trunks. Being engulfed in and carried by a wave of powder might actually be fun if it weren't for the near-certain chance of being pounded by large, heavy objects on the way down.

Avalanches are most common in mountainous high-altitude terrain, where sparse forests, deep snowfalls, steep grades, and bright sunshine all work to send snow accumulations skidding downward. But snowslides can occur in the rolling hills of Vermont and the steep ridges of Northern Michigan too, and these may be even more dangerous because they frequently take victims by surprise. Even metal-roofed barns have been known to bury people and livestock when the mass of snow collected on their steeply pitched roofs reached the point where gravity overcame friction.

Generally snow depths greater than 3 feet should be considered potential avalanche conditions in hill country. Slides rarely occur at gentle angles of 25–30 degrees, regardless of snow depth. On slopes of 35–40 degrees there might be an occasional wave of loose snow washing downhill. At 45–50 degrees there will be frequent avalanches, particularly after heavy, fresh snowfalls. At 60 degrees or greater, the possibility of an avalanche looms constantly after every light snowfall, and such terrain is probably best avoided by snowshoers of any skill level.

Avoidance is the secret to remaining unburied in avalanche country. Beware of sunny southerly slopes, especially after a recent snowfall, because 2 feet of fresh powder can quickly compact to 6 inches of heavy, wet snow that slides over top of the existing hardpack in what old-timers know as a "slab slide." Be alert for curled-over cornices at the tops of high windswept ridges and ledges; these beautifully sculpted natural wonders are worth seeing, but they always break off under their own weight, and can initiate a full-blown avalanche. Walking on top of ridges where chances of a snowslide look good is a safer, if more tiring, way to negotiate avalanche country, but be aware that snow next to the edge of anything is precarious. Walking out onto a drifted cornice could result in your being the trigger for an ensuing avalanche.

FIRST-AID KITS

The mercury had already dropped to −7 degrees when the heavy blade of my survival knife skipped out of the deer neck I was notching to hang as wolf bait. Air hissed through my clenched teeth as the Buck's shaving-sharp edge sunk in midway through the first knuckle of my index finger, parting my knit wool glove liner as cleanly as if it had been scissored.

First-aid kits don't have to be fancy, just effective. Don't venture into the woods without one.

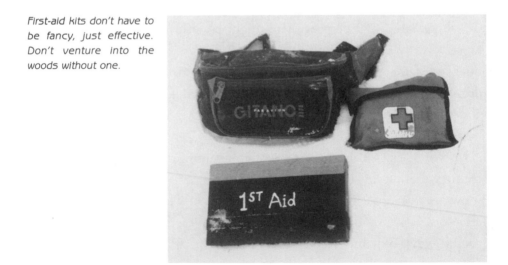

This wound would have been serious under any conditions, but there in a subzero swamp, alone and with three days till pickup, I faced a few more problems than I would have in summer. Most critical was stopping the blood loss from my half-severed appendage, because this was neither a good time nor place to be leaking vital fluids. But I also had to cope with necrosis, a dying off of injured tissue common in extreme cold, and the possibility of gangrene resulting from that.

A first-aid kit is like any other good insurance policy: You hope never to use it, yet dare not be without one. Following is a list of items that my own experiences have shown to be generic to every snowshoer's first-aid kit.

Daypacking & Fastpacking:
    1 roll of 0.5-inch self-adhesive safety tape
    1 small tube of triple-antibiotic ointment
    1 dozen aspirin
    1 dozen ibuprofen caplets, 200 mg
    2 air-activated chemical handwarmer packets
    1 tweezer
    1 toenail clipper
    1 package of moleskin for blisters
    10 feet of parachute cord or equivalent
    1 carry case (mine is a see-through videotape case)

Backpacking: Add to all of the above:
    1 dozen multivitamins
    1 tube of Ora-Gel or equivalent
    1 roll of 1-inch safety tape
    2 additional chemical handwarmer packets
    2 doses of a preferred laxative
    1 carry case (mine is a small fanny pack)

Don't stop with this list. The beauty of building your own medical kit is that it can be tailored to a specific environment and activity better than a typical store-bought first-aid kit. If you do opt for a manufactured first-aid kit, go through its contents and add to or subtract from them as you think necessary. Too many people—some of them my companions—have popped open their first-aid kits in time of need to find nothing of value. Never blindly trust any ready-made medical kit to have everything you'd want it to carry.

6

Orienteering on Snow

Sweat ran into my eyes as I took a compass bearing in the snow-bound forest near Michigan's Straits of Mackinac. I was scheduled to meet biologists from the Little Traverse Bay Bands of Odawa Indians at the Carp River the following morning, and night was already beginning to fall. I'd opted to shortcut 2 miles from the 7-mile trek by snowshoeing cross-country through cedar swamp, over tangled deadfalls of timber-sized trees uprooted by the Straits' sometimes vicious nor'westers. I knew the area as well as any man still living, but a foot of fresh powder atop 3 feet of standing hardpack had made forest landmarks difficult to identify.

Snowshoers require good orienteering equipment and the skills to use it perhaps more than any other outdoorsmen. Like shifting sand, wind-driven snow can reshape or even erase entire

Snowshoers require good orienteering equipment and the skills to use it perhaps more than any other outdoorsmen.

landscapes in just hours, and places you thought you knew intimately can become unrecognizable. But unlike any desert, ground cover in snow country is refreshed periodically with new layers from the sky, so the terrain changes almost constantly. Landmarks and trails may disappear, and places that are familiar in summer can become alien landscapes overnight.

In most snowshoeing scenarios getting lost is difficult because you can at least backtrack your own trail—but never count on that. Under blizzard conditions snow and wind can erase a trail in just a few minutes, so don't ever rely solely on backtracking to get you out of the woods. Add to that no sense of direction—a uniquely human trait—and people have gotten lost for days in areas smaller than some shopping malls.

COMPASS BASICS

Regardless of how ornate it might appear, its price tag, or how many on-board tools it carries, every compass does only one thing by itself: It points toward the magnetic north pole. Every other orienteering trick, from sophisticated triangulation techniques to just verifying your direction of travel, is based on first knowing the direction of magnetic north.

Probably the most important thing to remember about orienteering is to take a bearing before you venture off a beaten path. You can't know which direction leads out if you don't know which direction brought you in. The best bearing points are large, hard-to-miss landmarks like roads, railroad grades, rivers, or packed trails—something you can be sure to cross at some point on the way back.

Taking a bearing simply means aligning the compass dial and indicator with north, then using the dial to determine which directions you're coming from and going to. To take a bearing, hold the compass flat in your palm, parallel to the earth, and rotate its directional ring, or bezel, until the *N* on its face is in agreement with the north (usually red) half of the indicator. With the indicator and bezel so aligned, east is to the right, west to the left, and south to the rear.

Trust your compass. Believing that a compass is somehow "off" is a common mistake in the deep, untracked woods. The problem derives from a human reluctance to admit that we have no sense of direction. When a cross-country snowshoer does a quick compass check and discovers that the heading he's on has changed considerably since the last bearing, it can seem that a compass is lying. The simple truth is that a compass cannot be wrong; it can only point toward the magnetic north pole or be broken, and the latter is usually obvious.

In most snowshoeing scenarios a simple liquid-filled "pocket" compass that shows you the four directions is all that's needed. There are few places left where you can walk in a straight line for more than a few miles without encountering a road, railroad grade, or other large, hard-to-miss landmark. Also, it's difficult to accurately sight on a distant landmark when deep forest limits visibility to 100 feet or so.

Brunton's basic Tag-A-Long ($6) and Silva's Type 12 ($7) are both fine all-around compasses, and these should be treated as the valuable instruments they are, regardless of price. Despite the name, I recommend tying your pocket compass to a stout cord (spare bootlace) and wearing it around your neck every second, even while sleeping. Think of it as your guarantee of getting back home.

In mountain country, where you can see large identifiable landmarks from many miles distant, a more precise sighting compass like the Nexus Ranger Pro ($60) is a better choice. With a good prismatic sighting compass a snowshoer atop a tall peak can determine his precise location by triangulating from known landmarks, then get a bearing from one of them to follow before dropping back into lowland forest.

Deep woods and forest usually negate the advantages of a precision compass, reducing it to little more than a bulky pocket compass. But one, Brunton's new 8099 Eclipse ($80), has been specifically designed to do perform in all environments, from taking a quick bearing in tangled cedar swamp to precisely sighting on mountain peaks to locate a pass. Brunton put five years' worth of effort into creating the Eclipse, and based on personal experience with it in the field the 8099 sets a new standard for sporting compasses.

The Nexus Ranger Pro compass.

The Brunton 8099 Eclipse compass.

MAP BASICS

In the days of Lewis and Clark there were no maps to speak of, and virtually none that could be relied on for land navigation. The best an American frontiersman could manage was a simple, heavy brass-and-glass compass, and even those weren't common. Rivers, mountains, and valleys had yet to receive names that European immigrants could understand, and thousands of square miles had yet to see a boot track. Trade routes habitually kept to riverbanks, ridges, and other more easily followed geographic features. It was much harder to give a stranger directions to anywhere than it is now.

Today virtually every mile of our globe has been transferred in pictorial form to paper, and savvy snowshoers should never deny themselves the advantages of knowing what to expect from a place before actually going there. With a map and compass, you can know exactly (depending on how detailed your map is) what lies ahead and around long before reaching a place, and use that information to select the safest and easiest route. For the first time in history an explorer can be intimately familiar with a place that he has never seen. Early Americans could only have wished for such a potentially lifesaving advantage.

Using a map and compass together is simple. Lay the map on a flat surface, lay the compass on top, and orient both to north. If you can determine your general position on the map, it can then be used as a pictorial guide to lakes, roads, and other terrain features relative to your location.

MAGNETIC DECLINATION

Magnetic north is the direction that every compass must point toward. Unfortunately, the magnetic north pole and "true" north, to which most maps are oriented, aren't always in the same place on our planet. Some places, like Ishpeming, Michigan, are situated so that the poles are in alignment, meaning that the difference between map and compass is zero and can be ignored. In other places, like Fairbanks, Alaska, the difference between map north and compass north can be greater than 30 degrees. The effect of not compensating for just 3 degrees of declination would put a snowshoer off course by a quarter-mile after 5 miles of trekking. Again, this isn't usually a problem for dayhikers whose back trail intersects a road or some other large, hard-to-miss landmark, but if you're looking for a secluded cabin or campsite in heavy snow, it pays to be as close to dead-on as possible.

Correcting for differences between magnetic and true north poles is simple. Using the declination map shown here, first determine your approximate geographic position within the U.S. Then, using the numbered lines of declination as a guide, estimate how many degrees must be added or subtracted to make compass agree with map. If your location is west, or left, of the zero line, subtract the number of degrees shown from your compass heading. If you're east of the zero line, add those degrees to your bearing.

Compass-friendly maps with gridlines that are already adjusted to compensate for declination can be purchased from the United States Geographical Survey for $3 each. Or you can convert the gridlines yourself with ruler and pencil, the way Boy Scouts are still taught to do. Most map compasses, like the Brunton 8040, have adjustable bezels to compensate for declination, meaning you can adjust the compass itself to read directly and correctly from a true-north map.

Magnetic Declination Map of the United States

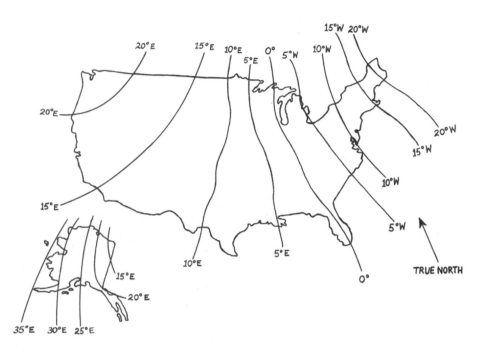

Add the number of degrees indicated on the map to the compass reading if you are east of the zero declination line. Subtract if you are west of the zero declination line.

GPS BASICS

I like the Global Positioning System when it works as advertised, but I must repeat the same warning found in the owner's manual of every GPS unit made: Do not use this instrument as your primary means of navigation.

The advantages of a GPS are numerous. So long as the unit can lock onto stationary-orbit satellites, it can determine its location on the planet to within 100 yards, or less, using the Universal

Map Coordinate system. A GPS can "waypoint," or remember, dozens of points of interest, then lead you back to and from those places with its "trek" mode.

Disadvantages are also numerous. Battery life is often less than 20 hours, especially in cold weather. Exposure to hard rain or falling into a river can take the unit out of commission indefinitely, and it's sometimes difficult to maintain a satellite lock in forest through even a leafless canopy. One cold night when we really could have used a waypoint, my companion's GPS simply refused to turn on at all (frost on the battery connections). My advice is to use your compass for navigation and your GPS for confirmation, for marking points of interest, and for convenience.

NATURAL COMPASSES

I've always thought it unfair that ours is virtually the only species on earth with no natural sense of direction. Mammals, birds, fish, even butterflies have a magnetic deposit in their noses and beaks that tells them continuously in which direction north lies. The animals don't know north from south in a human sense, but being able to home in on a single, fixed point gives them a stable bearing from which to travel, much the same as a snowshoer's compass. We humans also have a magnetic deposit in our noses, but anthropologists claim that it has never worked as a compass. If humans ever did have a sense of direction, the number of folks lost in the woods every year is proof enough that we've lost it.

But humans have a capacity for logic, and that can more than compensate for our sensory failings. The most important rule to remember is that wherever you are on earth, if that place is north of the equator, our sun must pass from east to west across the southern sky. The farther north you travel, the lower and more

A towering pine tree can help point hikers in the right direction.

southerly will be the sun's position on the horizon. In Australia, south of the equator, the opposite is true, with the sun always on the northern horizon.

Like sailors of old, snowshoers can also use stars in the heavens to guide their course at night, and you don't need to be an astronomer. Orion's Belt is one of the most obvious star groups in the winter sky. I've never been sharp at recognizing the shapes folks tell me are formed by stars, but Orion's Belt has guided me over many a night trail. Ostensibly the belt of Orion the Hunter, whom I cannot make out, the three stars that form it appear brightest in winter. They are always in the southern sky—southeast to be more precise—running in a diagonal from lower left to upper right.

Ursa Major and Ursa Minor (Latin for "big bear" and "little bear"), known generally as the Big and Little Dippers, are perhaps the most recognizable constellations. The Big Dipper, which of course resembles a water dipper, sits low in the northern sky in winter, its dipper shape vertical, with its handle pointing at the ground. The Little Dipper is to the Big Dipper's left (west) and oriented opposite, with its handle pointing upward, its dipper downward. Polaris, the North Star, is located at the tip of the Little Dipper's handle, and true to its name, this brightest of stars is always in the northern sky.

Our moon also indicates direction. Like the sun, a risen moon

The Winter Sky
Looking North
Jan 1. 8 p.m.   Dec 15. 9 p.m.   Dec 1. 10 p.m.   Nov 15. 11 p.m.   Nov 1 12 p.m.

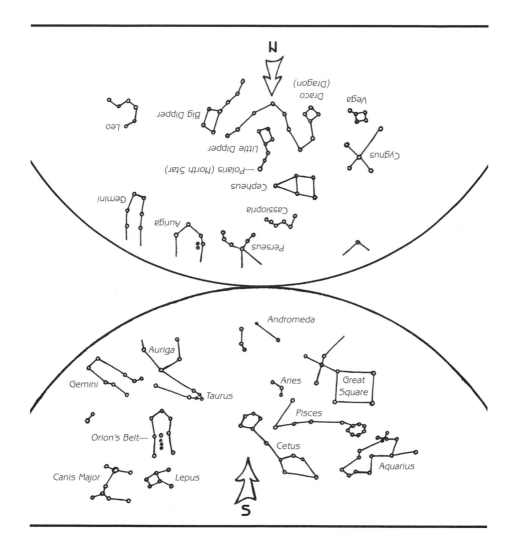

The Winter Sky
Looking South
Jan 1. 8 p.m.   Dec 15. 9 p.m.   Dec 1. 10 p.m.   Nov 15. 11 p.m.   Nov 1 12 p.m.

will always appear south of any location in the Northern Hemisphere, and it too crosses the sky from east to west. If you're snowshoeing directly toward a risen moon in any phase, you're headed south, which puts west on your right and east on your left.

Some trees can be used as directional indicators in windswept places. In the north, cold winter winds kill off branches and buds exposed to the brunt of seasonal nor'westers. That leaves the tallest pines with branches growing only on the leeward, or southeasterly, side of their tops. Only trees that face the full fury of icy prevailing winds exhibit this growth pattern, so if you see a tall spruce whose top is naked on one side, it's a sure bet that branches growing from the opposite side are pointing northeast.

Moss is not a reliable indicator of direction, although the old myth about it growing only or mostly on the north side of tree trunks is tougher to eradicate than the common cold. It is true that mosses tend to favor shade, and since the sun is always in the southern sky anywhere in the Northern Hemisphere, it seems logical that moss would favor a tree's northern face. The holes in that theory are northerly winds in winter that kill moss as well as young tree branches, and the fact that the damp, dense places favored by mosses are usually shaded enough to permit them to completely encircle a host tree's trunk.

Clouds and the winds that drive them across the sky are another predictable method for determining direction. In winter the prevailing winds across the U.S. and Canada are from the northwest, so clouds moving across the sky are on a southeasterly heading. Ground winds cannot be used in that way because valleys and hills can funnel prevailing winds into any direction, but high clouds moving across the winter sky are a reliable compass.

7

Staying Warm

I grew up in Northern Michigan, where lake-effect snows and the "Canadian Clipper," a finger of arctic air drawn southward into the Great Lakes region, make for winters that can kill a person just for standing around. I've watched the outer layers of skin peel from my fingertips during the weeks-long recovery from frostbite. I probably should have lost all my toes when I froze them solid (literally) while snowmobiling in my teenage years. Twice I've experienced the oddly seductive sleepiness that can overcome victims in the latter stages of hypothermia—after a period of considerable pain—and both were experiences I don't ever want to repeat.

A snowshoer's need to remain warm is no less than with any winter activity, but snow walkers face different challenges than skiers or snowmobilers. A dayhiker on snowshoes might be sweating profusely one moment as he claws his way to the top of a steep ridge, then face a stiff subzero wind in open country on the other side. Because a snowshoer's clothing needs will routinely range from one extreme to another, he requires an outfit with enough versatility to meet a broad range of needs.

PRINCIPLES OF INSULATION

When it comes to winter apparel, the advice heard most often is to dress in layers, yet I've never heard a one-minute public service announcement really explain just how you should go about doing that. Without specifics it's possible, even likely, that folks who attempt to follow such sketchy advice will end the day shivering with a case of hypothermia. The following sections deal with the nuts and bolts of putting together an effective layered snowshoeing outfit that performs as well on warm, sunny days as it will in −60 windchills. It just might have to.

Key to any insulation's effectiveness is "dead air," one or more layers of relatively motionless warmed air trapped between two or more layers of nonabsorbent insulating material. Motionless air blocks the passage of heat very well, yet allows moisture in vapor form to pass freely through, so moisture naturally migrates to the outer clothing. Every good insulation possesses those properties, but not all are suitable for garments—you wouldn't want to wear a sweater woven from fiberglass home insulation.

The ideal cold-weather outfit confines as much body heat as possible within those dead-air layers, while simultaneously passing through all the moisture generated through perspiration. If your clothing doesn't retain enough dead air, you'll get cold; if it retains too much moisture, you'll get cold. To avoid these scenarios, each layer of clothing a snowshoer wears should perform a different yet complementary function.

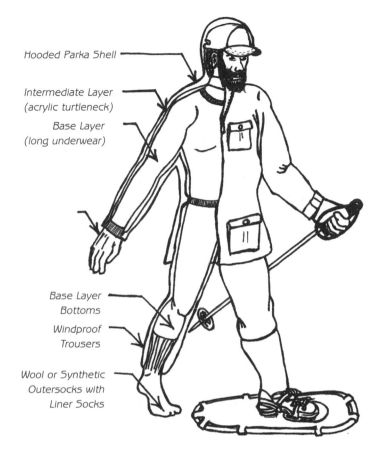

Hooded Parka Shell

Intermediate Layer
(acrylic turtleneck)

Base Layer
(long underwear)

Base Layer
Bottoms

Windproof
Trousers

Wool or Synthetic
Outersocks with
Liner Socks

Cutaway drawing of a Layered snowshoeing outfit.

The advantage of a layered snowshoeing outfit is that garments can be removed and added as needed, or mixed and
matched to suit whatever environmental conditions you might encounter. Again, you'll need a working-sized day- or fanny pack to
stash what you aren't wearing, but you'll be fully prepared for anything from a blizzard with −60 windchills (dangerous) to an unsea-
sonably warm rain (more dangerous). I've seen both, once or twice
in the same day, and both conditions have killed experienced outdoorsmen who weren't prepared to meet them.

BASE LAYERS

No component of any cold-weather outfit is more critical than a proper base layer, the garment that will be in constant direct contact with your skin. A functional base layer must be nonabsorbent to allow free passage of moisture vapors to the outside; it must hold in as much body heat as possible; and it must be comfortable enough to wear for long periods of heavy activity without chafing.

Because it absorbs and holds perspiration moisture, thereby displacing warmed air, cotton is the worst choice for long underwear. Cotton "thermal" long underwear is both common and inexpensive in most department stores, but no purchase is a good deal if the product doesn't perform. Cotton doesn't—a fact that becomes obvious after sweat-soaked cotton causes you to start shivering from loss of body heat through evaporation.

Woolen long johns remain a perennial favorite with folks who spend a lot of time out of doors in snowy weather. But despite wool's natural ability to repel water and to trap warmed air, many find woolies to be uncomfortably scratchy against bare skin. A pair of boxer or athletic shorts worn under the bottoms helps prevent chafing between the thighs, a common irritation on long treks. An old trick I used during my boyhood was to wear a cotton T-shirt that was a size or two too small under my woolen long-john top. Stretched taut, the T-shirt absorbed much less moisture than it otherwise would have while providing welcome protection against scratchiness. Better yet is a lightweight synthetic (rayon, acrylic, polyester . . .) turtleneck worn under the woolie top.

Polypropylene "fleece," a soft and water-repellent fabric comprised entirely of plastic fibers, was the first to prove itself just as good an insulation as wool for long underwear. Military surplus polypros (often "mil-spec" look-alikes) retail for about $35 a set. Again, low or no cotten content is best, so read the labels before you buy. Authentic polypropylene or acrylic GI long johns can keep you warm when wet, and they dry quickly.

The best base layer I've found yet is the new Tek-1 outfit from Performance Sports Apparel of Reading, Pennsylvania. Made from the company's patented Intera fabric, these garments literally draw, not just wick, moisture away from the skin. They can go from underwater to completely dry in one-third the time of other synthetics (about 60 minutes), which means that your skin remains drier during periods of heavy perspiration. I've snowshoed more than 100 miles in mine so far and worn them camping in ambient temps down to −15 (−25 windchill), and I'm a believer. Perhaps most attractive is the company's guarantee that Intera will never lose its wicking ability, no matter how

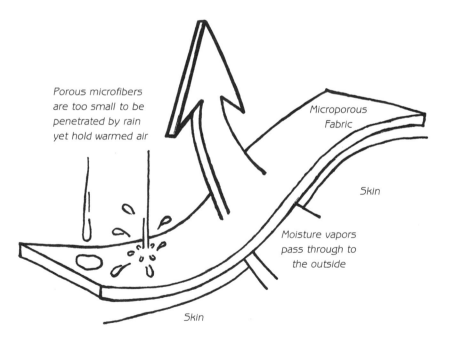

Porous microfibers are too small to be penetrated by rain yet hold warmed air

Microporous Fabric

Skin

Moisture vapors pass through to the outside

Skin

Tek-1 base layer. No component of any cold-weather outfit is more critical than a proper base layer.

many times it's laundered. Prices average about $30 for the drawers and $40 for a nice zip-neck turtleneck top that can be worn opened or closed as conditions demand.

A less expensive long john I've liked well is Duofold's Variterm™ Thermastat line. I really came to appreciate mine about a year back in March, when 20-degree temperatures and a hard rain combined to first saturate then glaze everything in a sheath of ice. I hiked 6 miles in that misery before arriving at camp, where I spent the night. I credit my Varitherm underwear with keeping that potentially hypothermic environment from becoming more than an inconvenience. Retail is about $25 each for drawers and crew-neck top.

INTERMEDIATE LAYERS

Covering the base layer are intermediate layers. Here, kept from touching your skin by a soft nonabsorbent base layer, is where that scratchy wool cable-knit sweater works great. Worn without a shell layer during periods of heavy exertion, a knit sweater breathes well enough to dissipate large amounts of moisture and keep its wearer cool. If the cooling effect becomes too great, just throw on a light windproof shell and the sweater becomes a thick layer of trapped, warmed air.

Sweaters can be expensive, but resale outlets often provide a treasure trove of sometimes high-quality sweaters that someone gave as a gift to somebody who didn't want it. Sweaters aren't nearly as stylish as they once were, and I frequently walk out with a functional like-new wool or synthetic knit sweater (retail $40–50) for under $5.

I also recommend an insulated button-up overshirt. This shirt functions essentially as a jacket liner for very cold weather, worn over base and intermediate layers to provide another layer of insulating air. It also provides another option for mixing and matching your outfit to suit a given type of weather. Department store versions retail for around $15, and work great for snowshoeing or camping, but I have a $40 Thinsulate-lined shirt from L. L. Bean that I consider a permanent part of my snowshoeing daypack.

SHELL LAYERS

This is the layer that armors you against the elements. A good shell layer stops subzero winds from reaching and whisking away the body heat beneath. It refuses to let water seep through, yet allows free passage of warmed moisture in vapor form to the outside.

Because it is the wind- and waterproof layer, a proper shell must seal out the elements as thoroughly as is practical. It must have a hood, because crossing a frozen lake or large open space nearly always means exposure to subzero windchills, and its zipper should be heavy, backed up by an overflap with snaps. Breast pockets should be large, with even larger hip pockets to accommodate gloves and hats. A cinch cord around the inside waist works to further isolate body heat around the torso. Length should reach past the buttocks, preferably with an elastic drawstring around the bottom hem. Zippered vents at the armpits are very helpful for letting off steam, so to speak, when physical exertions become strenuous enough to prompt sweating.

Gore-Tex is usually the fabric of choice for parka shells because it's both waterproof and breathable, a valuable and potentially lifesaving feature should you run into a cold unseasonable rain miles from civilization. Good Gore-Tex shells retail for about $200 and up from name-brand manufacturers like Columbia Sports-wear, L. L. Bean, and The North Face.

"Water-repellent" (that is, leaky, cold, and uncomfortable in the rain) shells can be made virtually waterproof with two or three light applications of Tent & Gear Proof spray from NikWax. Tent seam sealer applied to open seams—those not covered by a rolled-over hem (hood and shoulders, usually)—prevents water from penetrating those potential leak points.

Tent & Gear Proof is not recommended for breathable fabrics because it works by sealing pores in the fabric, which of course defeats their purpose. Gore-Tex and Sympatex are best treated with NikWax's TX-Direct spray, which is made for breathable fabrics but works as a good general-purpose waterproofing treatment in its own right. Sixteen-ounce pump-spray bottles of Tent & Gear Proof and TX-Direct retail for $17 and $21, respectively.

SOCKS

Technology has improved virtually every aspect of snowshoeing, and none of it more so than socks. No longer must snowshoers suffer scratchy, coarse woolies that could wear hide from the feet almost as fast as a bad pair of boots. Today's socks are soft—even slippery—against their wearer's skin, cushiony enough to provide a snug fit between foot and boot, and absorb almost no moisture.

Modern pac boots have greatly diminished the amount of warmth a snowshoer needs from his socks, but some things remain unchanged. Never wear cotton socks, as perspiration-soaked cotton helps defeat even the warmest pac boot. Never put plastic bags over your socks, because that archaic practice cancels out any breathability your socks or boots might have, and will actually make your feet feel wetter and colder.

My favorite winter sock system is essentially the same as the liner-and-oversock combination that works so well in hiking boots, but heavier. I'm hooked on WigWam's Merino wool liners with one of their winter-weight wool-blend oversocks. Aside from wicking perspiration away from the feet, they provide a nearly friction-free environment, as well as enough padding to allow a snug fit between boot and foot. Liners retail for about $6 a pair, but ordinary polyester dress socks will also work well, though these tend to wear out more quickly. Winter-weight oversocks are priced at about $12 a pair.

Do avoid making the common mistake of putting on too many pairs of socks, even good ones. Too many socks can squeeze your feet, hampering blood flow and making your feet colder than they would be if you wore only a single pair.

FOOTWEAR

Like good socks, a proper pair of snowshoe boots will go a long way toward making any outing more enjoyable. First, I do not recommend any boot for snowshoeing that isn't a pac boot with a (usually) removable liner. Insulated hiking boots made for snowshoeing are simply not warm enough for more than an hour or two of activity. If you're on the trail after sunset, when temperatures can plummet 20 degrees in as many minutes, it's a good bet that your toes will suffer without adequate boots.

My criteria for a snowshoeing boot include a comfort rating of at least −40 degrees, −100 when I'm backpacking for several days at a time and must rise each morning to frozen footwear. Liners should be removable because I wear them in my sleeping bag on very cold nights, and because I rotate them with a spare set from my pack should they become wet. The uppers must reach at least mid-calf to keep pant legs out of the snow and to protect shins from being barked or stabbed by branches. Soles should have large, self-cleaning lugs with prominent heels, and preferably a molded step at the rear of each heel to hold your snowshoes' heel straps in place.

Not many years ago pac boots were heavy and bulky, clumsy in places where agility was needed, and prone to chewing up the feet of those who tried to hike long distances in them. Ice fishermen, deer hunters, and snowmobilers didn't mind, but snowshoers and winter hikers needed a boot made for walking many miles on snow. We got them; following are the boots I've liked best on snowshoes.

DAYHIKING BOOTS

Pac-boot manufacturers are still trying for a perfect winter boot, but there have been some impressive attempts in recent years. I've put over 100 miles on a pair of Rocky's Ozark guide boots ($120), and in temperatures down to 10 degrees these integral-liner boots can snowshoe or hike with the best of them. The Ozark is impervious to snow and a quick dunking, though it isn't waterproof enough for wading. I especially like it in early spring, when terrain can vary from deep snow and ice to mud and flowing water but temperatures don't warrant the extra warmth and bulk of a full-blown pac boot.

PAC BOOTS

For really cold temps—down to zero and below—I don't fool around: I wear a boot rated for –100 degrees. My favorite extreme-cold snowshoe boots are La Crosse's knee-high Winter-Breaker ($180), Sorel's cushy Alaska ($150), and Rocky's ultralight Snow Stalker ($130), in that order. I like the aggressive traction provided by a semirigid lug sole, as well as the armorlike protection they provide from sharp ice and shin-busting tree branches.

If you're not going to be kicking around a campfire, and if you prefer traditional-style footwear, mukluks from the Steger company of Ely, Minnesota (800-685-5857) are an attractive option. All are built on thick moosehide lowers with bonded rubber tractor-tread soles that give with contours in the trail. The result is sneakerlike comfort with good traction, and feet that stay warm because they are in effect being massaged by bumps and irregularities underfoot. Steger doesn't assign comfort ratings, but I've grown fond of their Yukon Jack mukluk ($130), and my wife field-tested both their Navajo ($230) and Yukon Kate ($120) models for my fourth book, *The Outdoors Almanac*. Neither of us has ever gotten cold feet, but it is important that any of them be waterproofed before exposure to snow (see below).

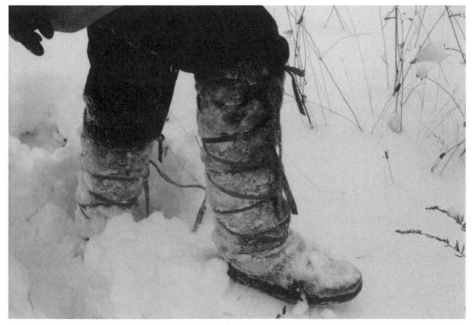

Mukluks give sneakerlike comfort with good traction and warmth. These are Steger Navajo mukluks.

Kids generally love snowshoeing, but the typical children's pac boot is a less-than-serious attempt to keep its wearer's feet warm. The one exception, and the only boot I've judged fit enough for my granddaughter to wear so far, is Sorel's Kids' Super-Warm Glacier. Essentially a downsized version of the adult model with the same name, the mukluk-style Glacier is comfort-rated to a respectable −60 degrees. It has a removable ThermoPlus liner, an insulating midsole, and the durability I'd expect from a Sorel.

SNOWSHOE-BOOT MAINTENANCE

Compared to the mud, sharp rock, and sand that hiking boots must routinely cope with, snow is relatively easy on foot gear. Snow doesn't melt against the outside of a good pac boot (if it does, you're losing heat), so external moisture isn't a big problem, and few surfaces are less abrasive than snow.

Nonetheless, pac boots require at least some care if their owner intends to get as much service out of them as possible. A foot in the mud is possible in winter, even on snowshoes, leaving abrasive, acidic particles in seams, on stitching, and over breathable fabric panels. Care must also be taken with natural rubber lowers and soles, which can become weatherchecked (cracked) just like a car tire if not protected from ultraviolet rays.

Snowshoeing boots should be treated, at minimum, at the beginning of winter and again just before they're put away in spring. Begin by washing off grit and dust with a good boot cleaner, like Thompson's Oil Soap or one of NikWax's several footwear cleaners, working the cleaner into seams and crevices with an old toothbrush. Any detergent will work, but dedicated footwear cleaners are designed to remove grit and grime without also removing waterproofing and protective treatments already there.

For weatherproofing grain-type boot leathers, I prefer Liquid NikWax. For suede leathers, like the moosehide used in Steger's mukluks, my favorite is Snow-Proof rubberized silicone spray. Fabric ventilation panels are treated with NikWax's spray-on TX Direct, which causes the Cordura to repel water, but doesn't affect the breathability of Gore-Tex panels beneath them.

Rubber lowers are best treated with a good silicone product. Automotive silicone sprays found in department stores work to keep rubber from aging, but I've really liked the results I get from Armor-All, the same stuff used to make tires look new and dashboards shine. Be warned that silicone is extremely slippery, and take care not to apply it to boot soles or get it on a floor.

HANDWEAR

Hands and fingers are perhaps the most exercised parts of the body. Like a bodybuilder's biceps, the skin over them feels relatively thin because there is little or no fat between it and the underlying muscle. Since fat functions as an insulator, that means there is little protection from the cold for these fragile but vital appendages.

Good handwear is a must for every snowshoer. On the trail, where I use and need my hands and fingers more or less constantly, I prefer a rugged pair of gloves. Mittens retain more heat than gloves because they shield the entire hand instead of isolating each finger and are better for long, stationary waits behind camera or binocular.

A system I've used for many years is a Well-Lamont leather glove shell ($12) worn over a knit woolen or synthetic liner that can be quickly replaced by spare liners from the day- or backpack. This system, a variation of the U.S. Army's, provides sufficient warmth for snowshoeing in temps down to −10 (for me, at least), with enough dexterity to operate a camera, work snowshoe bindings, or squeeze a

trigger. If a more sensitive feel is required, or if the weather is relatively mild, either shells or liners may be worn by themselves as
conditions demand.

A new superwarm glove system I've used and liked is the
Gronland from Well-Lamont's Hotfingers subsidiary. This two-
piece system consists of a nylon gauntlet-type shell with rubberized
palm and ComforTemp Dynamic Climate Control (DCC) insulation over a polypropylene fleece liner. The shell glove has a quick-
release cinch strap over the wrist and a cord-lock-type drawstring at
the forearm to keep out snow and further seal heat inside. Either
shell or liner may be worn alone as conditions dictate, or you can
wear them together for near-mitten warmth in temperatures below
zero. The Gronland retails for about $40.

For extremely cold weather (−20 degrees and lower), or for
relatively sedentary activities like ice fishing and wildlife observa-
tion, I sometimes replace the glove shells with a pair of loose-fitting
gauntlet-length mittens. Glove liners and mitten shells will keep
your hands warm in almost any weather, and a mitten can be
quickly pulled off when the fingers are needed, leaving them protected by a knit liner. Name-brand mittens made from modern
materials are available at a variety of prices, but GI surplus canvas
mitten shells ($15) and no-name imports made from rawhide with
synthetic pile lining ($10) are more than satisfactory.

HEADWEAR

Proper, functional headwear is a must for snowshoeing. In
sunny, bright weather where reflected glare can give snowshoers a
splintering headache, or even make them temporarily blind, I generally opt for a simple baseball cap. The cap's bill can be pulled low
to shade the eyes and keep them from squinting, and it works
much better with a hood than full-brimmed hats.

In very cold or windy weather I pocket the cap and don a full-face ski mask, rolled up like a tuque, or watchcap, or pulled down over my face as the weather demands. There are heavier and more expensive winter hats, but a simple, inexpensive knit mask or balaclava that covers the nose and mouth will be as much as most snowshoers will ever need, especially when worn under a parka shell hood.

REGULATING YOUR BODY TEMPERATURE

While layering your clothing in different combinations to match different weather conditions and activities is perhaps the most important trick to keeping warm, it isn't the only one. Hypoglycemia, or an abnormally low blood-sugar level, is a common affliction among snowshoers and cross-country skiers, who might burn a day's worth of calories in just a couple of hours.

Studies conducted by Ball State University show that snowshoers burn 400 to more than 1,000 calories per hour, depending on terrain, snow, and activity levels—or about twice the energy expenditure of a runner over the same distance. The result is that a working snowshoer's available blood sugars can run low quicky, forcing the body to run at a slower pace that doesn't generate sufficient heat to maintain warmth. The solution is an ample supply of high-calorie, complex-carbohydrate finger foods like granola bars, cheese, and summer sausage stashed in a daypack. Each of these provides a quick energy boost with simple sugars, as well as slower-burning complex carbohydrates for long-lasting energy.

As logic suggests, burning lots of calories means expending lots of physical energy, and that generally means elevated body temperatures. Perspiration is an enemy that should be avoided as much as is possible, because wet clothing is the quickest route to hypothermia.

A good rule of thumb is to dress as lightly as possible while actively 'shoeing. If you begin to feel overheated, first remove your headwear. Head wounds bleed profusely because a high volume of blood flows through the scalp, which also means that a disproportionate amount of body heat is emitted from an uncovered head. A simple knit ski mask, recommended earlier, is my winter hat of choice because it can be adjusted to cover more or less of the head, or just stuffed into a pocket.

Likewise your hands. Leather glove shells can be removed during periods of heavy activity, leaving knit liners to protect the fingers. Or you might opt to remove your gloves altogether. In rougher terrain I often wear only the shells, more for protection than for warmth.

Higher-end parka shells have ventilation zippers, sometimes called "pit vents," at the armpits. Many snowshoers fail to recognize the value of a shell with armpit ventilation, but if you open those vents to whatever degree is most comfortable, you can snowshoe for hours without sweating noticeably.

A trick that has been used with good results for many years by savvy deer hunters in the North is the "kidney warmer." As the name suggests, this item is essentially just a source of heat applied over the kidneys in the lumbar region of the back. All blood in the body flows through the kidneys once every four minutes, so applying a source of constat heat in that area effectively spreads warmth through the entire body.

The first kidney warmers I saw used two fuel-stick handwarmers in an elastic waist belt. Then we started duct-taping air-activated handwarmer packets to our undershirts. Now you can buy self-adhesive air-activated kidney warmers for about $2 at some sporting goods stores.

WINDCHILL FACTORS

I don't put much stock in windchill factors, although they are popular with relatives in southern states who frequently call to ask about the weather whenever I'm out shoveling snow. Weather forecasters like to emphasize windchills for the air of danger they lend to hourly news reports, but the cooling effects of wind are largely overrated.

That's not to say that a windchill factor of −40 degrees isn't dangerous—it is—but a smart snowshoer guards against its cooling effects. A windproof hooded shell virtually negates windchill when crossing open country, but the time-honored rule of thumb for wind is to get out of it whenever possible. Stay inside the sheltered tree line along lakeshores and in open country, or on the leeward side of ridges and other natural obstructions, and windchill factors become inconsequential.

Except where bragging rights are concerned. Because most folks who ask how your snowshoe outing went will be more interested in knowing windchill rather than ambient temperatures, the following conversion chart might well become the most referenced section of this book.

Windchill Chart												
Temperature (°F)												
35	30	25	20	15	10	5	0	-5	-10	-15	-20	-25
Wind (mph)												
05	32	27	22	16	11	6	0	−5	−10	−15	−21	−26	−31
10	22	16	10	3	−3	−9	−15	−22	−27	−34	−40	−46	−52
15	16	9	2	−5	−11	−18	−25	−31	−38	−45	−51	−58	−65
20	12	4	−3	−10	−17	−24	−31	−39	−46	−53	−60	−67	−74
25	8	1	−7	−15	−22	−29	−36	−44	−51	−59	−66	−74	−81
30	6	−2	−10	−18	−25	−33	−41	−49	−56	−64	−71	−79	−86
35	4	−4	−12	−20	−27	−35	−43	−52	−58	−67	−74	−82	−92
40	3	−5	−13	−21	−29	−37	−45	−53	−60	−69	−76	−84	−92

8

A Buyer's Guide
to Snowshoes

Snowshoeing became more popular in the late 1990s than it had been in all of the previous century. In hindsight, it was a matter of time before someone thought to exploit synthetic materials and new manufacturing technology in pursuit of a better snowshoe. When I was a kid there existed just four types of snowshoes that I knew: the tennis-racket-shaped Michigan, the egg-shaped bearpaw, the long and narrow Alaska, and the canoe-shaped Ojibwa. All were wooden-framed, decked with webbing of lacquered rawhide, and each one was created from the hands of a skilled craftsman whose name was burned or stamped into each frame.

No such simplicity exists for today's snowshoe shopper. There are about a dozen major snowshoe manufacturers in North America today, and just one of them, the Tubbs Snowshoe Company, offered 27 choices in 1999. Multiply that number, more or less, by the number of snowshoe manufacturers and you have a mind-boggling array of shapes, bindings, sizes, and other features to choose from. Because even avid enthusiasts can usually snowshoe only in their spare time, and because snowshoe designs are being re-engineered every year, it's getting tough to decide which brand and make is best suited to your needs. To help with the confusion of buying a new pair of snowshoes, I offer the following evaluations of snowshoes that I've personally tested in the field.

ATLAS 1033, 9"×29.5"

I consider this snowshoe to be one of the two best general-purpose models made today, and you'll find it strapped to the feet of more professional outdoorsmen than perhaps any other. With an area of 9"×29.5" the 1033 is adequate for any type or depth of snow, though a larger (and of course heavier) 'shoe with more flotation may be desired in deep fluff. Riveted Hypalon decking with reinforced tails—the area of most wear—and seam-welded aluminum frames make the 1033 an almost unbreakable workhorse of a snowshoe.

The 1033's binding is a simple but effective affair with Switchback™ straps that double back on themselves. This arrangement uses the straps' own tension to help keep them tight, taking much of the strain off quick-release buckles at the toes, instep, and heel. Traction is provided by aggressive stainless-steel cleats that offer firm footing on powder, hardpack, or glare ice. Properly tightened, this binding is one of the most stable and easiest to manipulate, though I still find it much easier to work the straps and buckles of this "glove-friendly" system barehanded.

The 1033 is rated to carry up to 275 pounds, although I prefer a larger snowshoe for loads of 250 pounds—even lighter if the

Atlas 1033 snowshoes.

trail is unbroken powder. Pair weight is an ultralight 4 pounds. A unique strap-around carrier makes transporting the 'shoes somewhat convenient, while being small enough to stuff into a pocket when the 1033s are on your feet. Retail is about $250.

ATLAS 1044, 9.5″×36″

This is essentially the same snowshoe as Atlas's 1033 above, except made larger with a surface area of 9.5″×36″ to provide more flotation on soft or fluffy snow. The 1044 has riveted Hypalon decking, welded frames, and Atlas's popular Switchback™ binding with stainless-steel crampons for sure footing. When the load is heavy, the trail unbroken, and the country unforgiving—or all of the above—this is the snowshoe I reach for first.

Like its smaller brother, the 1033, the 1044 has been engineered never to fail or break in the roughest backcountry. Besides being TiG welded at their joints, the frames are braced across their tails with a stout channel-shaped cross member welded to either side—a nice feature that is so far exclusive to Atlas. I've bridged my 1044s countless times while trail breaking through swamps, marshes, and deadfalls without so much as a creak, even though I could feel the frames flex perceptibly underfoot.

Rated to support 300 pounds, the 1044 is as much snowshoe as you'll ever need, and maybe a little more than most recreational snowshoers want. Weight is 5.1 pounds for the pair, which is light considering their strength. Retail is around $270.

GREAT BEAR SNOWSHOES

If you like the idea of crunching along winter trails on authentic wood-and-rawhide snowshoes just like those worn by trappers and Indians when America was a vast wilderness, Great Bear 'shoes might be what you're looking for. Individually handmade by craftsman Ron Amos of Kila, Montana, these are the most handsome snowshoes I've ever seen (almost too nice to wear). Each pair is hand-formed, fitted, and laced, and Amos uses cardboard cutouts of each customer's boots to guarantee a perfect match between 'shoes and 'shoer. Finished frames are serial-numbered with the inscription HAND CRAFTED BY RON AMOS, KILA, MT on one, and CUSTOM MADE FOR [CUSTOMER NAME] on the other.

While any of the Great Bear models would serve well as a wall

The "Mountain H" binding on a handmade Great Bear Enterprises snowshoe.

decoration, Amos's snowshoes are built to be absolutely reliable in the backcountry. His white ash frames are among the strongest I've seen, formed through a proprietary process in which the wood is boiled, not steamed like other traditional snowshoes. Decking is hand-laced rawhide sealed against the elements with three heavy coats of marine varnish, each of which has been allowed to cure for 48 hours before the next is applied. Bindings are Amos's own "Mountain H System," handmade from top-grain cowhide and fastened at toe, instep, and heel with solid-brass buckles.

Great Bear's model line covers all of the traditional styles: bearpaw, Huron (or Michigan), Alaska, Ojibwa, and New England (an elongated bearpaw). Weight and size of course vary for different models, but except for their lack of crampons each is comparable to synthetic 'shoes in the same load-bearing categories. Price for all models is $298.

LITTLE BEAR CUBS AND GRIZZLIES FOR KIDS

It wasn't lack of desire that used to keep kids from learning to snowshoe, but lack of snowshoes small enough to fit their feet. Little Bear Cubs and Grizzlies models solve that problem with a tough injection-molded polyethylene grid that serves as both frame and decking.

Cubs are designed for children two through five years old. Size is 6″×14″ and rated to carry up to 50 pounds. Weight for the pair is just 1 pound. Grizzlies are meant to fit kids five years and up— at least up to the 'shoes maximum carry rating of 100 pounds. Dimensions are 8.5″×16″ with a pair weight of 2.5 pounds.

Bindings for both models are unique and simple for little fingers to operate. Instead of a heel strap, the flexible molded one-piece polyethylene binding has a heel cup to arbitrarily position your little one's boot in the right place every time. Just push the boot as far rearward as it can go, tighten instep and toe straps, and turn your child loose for some of the best fun and safest exercise a youngster can have these days. Thumb-release buckles make Little Bears as easy to take off as they are to put on.

Grizzlies and Cubs are each available in five eye-catching (and hard-to-lose) colors: purple, royal blue, forest green, yellow, and hunter orange. Their grid decking provides outstanding traction on all types of snow, even on hills. If you want them outfitted for ice walking, either can be ordered with child-safe stainless-steel pegs (claws) inserted into their bottoms; seven for the Cubs, nine for the Grizzlies. Grizzlies retail for about $55, $40 for the Cubs.

MSR DENALI, 8"×30"

While I'll admit right off that Mountain Safety Research's Denali snowshoe is not my favorite snowshoe, it does have some attractive features, especially for beginners. First, the binding straps—three across the instep and one around the heel—are essentially very heavy, very tough rubber bands. The end of each instep strap is tipped with a disk that's larger than the buckle it goes through, so you never need to rethread the straps back through their buckles.

Fastening the Denali's bindings is a simple matter of inserting your boot and hooking the perforated strap over a mating projection on its buckle when the desired tightness is achieved. I do prefer a more secure binding when the route includes clambering over deadfallen trees or through a treacherous spring-fed swamp, even though my own Denali's bindings have proved remarkably stable in the rough stuff.

Because the Denali is an integrated design with one-piece injection-molded frame and deck made entirely of polyethylene plastic, it easily sheds snow and ice that can weigh down framed snowshoes. Steel toe crampons and traction rails riveted onto the unbreakable decking provide a good grip on steep grades, and the hinge-type binding pivot is comfortable, if a bit squeaky in subzero temperatures. The basic snowshoe is 8"×22" with a pair weight of 3.5 pounds, a load rating of 150 pounds in powder (200-plus on a packed trail), and a nice price tag of around $70.

"Flotation tails" that fasten securely onto three points at the Denali's rear and increase its load rating to 250 pounds are, I think, essential for making this a truly functional snowshoe, and I never remove mine. I recommend the longer 13.5-inch version, even though doing so adds another half-pound to each shoe and about $30 to the selling price. Being almost maintenance-free and nearly indestructible makes the Denali a good choice for the car trunk.

POWDER WINGS-LITE 10"×29" COLLAPSIBLE SNOWSHOE

If coolness can be considered a desirable quality for snowshoes, then the Powder Wings collapsible snowshoes win handsdown on that front. The frames consist of formed sections of aluminum tubing shock-corded together, much like a tent pole, that roll up and stow into a fanny pack (included). When assembled into a 10"×29" frame, the sections are held together by the tension of stout Hypalon decking that snaps in place over the tubing. With a little practice you should be able to assemble both shoes in around five minutes, even while wearing gloves. Pair weight for the Wings-Lite model is 4.8 pounds, and they're rated to carry up to 230 pounds.

Powder Wings lend themselves very well to the role of emergency survival snowshoes; the fanny-packed 'shoes can be tossed into a car trunk, bungeed to the rear of a snowmobile, or belted around a snowboarder's waist. And should you have need of them for getting to safety across deep snow, the large fanny pack your Powder Wings came out of is very handy for carrying spare clothing and other necessities.

The Powder Wings 7075 T-9 aluminum frames are said to be nearly equal to titanium in strength, but although mine have proven surprisingly unbreakable on some pretty rugged trails, these are not hard-core cross-country snowshoes. Toe and heel crampons offer traction good enough for glare ice, but the 'shoe's Summit Tracker binding is overcomplicated and needs occasional retightening on the trail. Despite these few minor flaws, though, I think Powder Wings-Lites are an ideal choice for motorists, snowmobilers, skiers, and snowboarders who can manage a $250 price tag.

REDFEATHER BACKCOUNTRY, 9.5"×36"

This is easily the most eye catching among synthetic 'shoes, with its yellow aluminum frame and the company's trademark red feather against a green mountain pattern on black Hypalon decking. The Backcountry 9.5"×36" trail-buster model is the largest of this series, weighing just over 6 pounds for the pair and rated to carry "over 220 pounds."

The Backcountry's EPIC binding is the type normally found on snowboards, essentially stiff polyurethane straps at heel, instep, and toe that slide into a mating quick-release buckle, then ratchet to the desired tightness—or more. This system is very secure and stable, and unlike most glove-friendly bindings it can be operated while actually wearing gloves. There is no slop between boot and 'shoe, and the binding has proved surprisingly ice-free in the field. If a buckle cannot be locked completely down because of ice build-up inside, just work the locking lever back and forth a few times until it does.

In terms of long-term wear, comfort, and maneuverability, the Backcountry is equal to top-of-the-line models from other manufacturers. Hypalon decking makes the 'shoes quiet on even crusted snow, and their aggressive aluminum crampons are epoxy powder-coated to help prevent ice buildup in winter and corrosion during summer storage. It isn't built so stoutly as Atlas's 1044 or Tubbs's Altitude, but it will carry its advertised load with no trouble, and with a price tag of $240 the Redfeather Backcountry is priced about $30 less.

SHERPA RU HIKER, 9"×30"

This is a very good general-purpose snowshoe that some say equals Atlas's 1033 in terms of real-world strength and performance. With a surface area of 9"×30," the RU Hiker is capable of handling any snow while carrying loads up to 230 pounds. Decking material is tough 1,050-denier nylon coated with PVC on the top and abrasion-resistant polyurethane on its bottom. Frames are strong aircraft-grade aluminum tubing, anodized instead of painted to help resist snow and ice buildup.

The RU Hiker's most popular feature is its Lotus Comfort™ binding, which uses a unique crisscross strap design to tighten the entire binding with only two buckles. Just step into the binding, position the heel and instep straps, and pull the free ends of the buckle straps at either side of your instep to tighten toe, instep, and heel simultaneously. This system is based on a sports medicine wrapping technique called the Calcanean Lock, used to brace and strengthen the ankle or wrist joints of professional athletes, and it's at least one of the best bindings yet invented.

Other features include a tapered design that allows the shoes to nest close to one another, aggressive aluminum toe and heel crampons, and a pair weight of less than 6 pounds. But the RU Hiker's best feature by far is its price tag, which averages $170.

SHERPA POOKA WALKER

This is the most impressive kid's 'shoe I've seen. The Pooka Walker is made with the same features I'd like to see in an adult snowshoe, except with appropriately smaller dimensions. An area of 7"×18" gives the 'shoe enough flotation to support 150 pounds on hardpack, 100 pounds on deep powder. Heavy 820-denier decking material is PVC-coated to prevent snow buildup, and riveted in 12 places to a sturdy tubular frame of 0.75-inch-diameter aluminum.

The Pooka Walker's binding is a simple affair that uses a drawstring lace system with a single slide-lock buckle to secure toe and instep. A pull against the slide-lock's release ring loosens both and is easy for little hands to work while wearing gloves or mittens. A single nylon strap with a quick-release buckle secures the heel. I was skeptical of this arrangement's reliability on the trail, but my fears that the laces would work loose proved to be unwarranted. The only modification I made was to tie the loose ends of the laces together above their slide-locks with a square knot. This makes the binding more kid friendly by adding a loop that can be pulled against with a finger when pushing the slide-lock tight.

The Pooka Walker's very effective crampons are a pivoting toe-plate of formed aluminum that grips steep grades and slippery ice as well as adult models. Despite concerns, metal crampons pose no danger to children, although I do recommend removing any sharp burrs along their stamped-out serrations with 50-grit sandpaper just to be safe. Weight is about 1.5 pounds for the pair, and retail averages $60.

TUBBS ALTITUDE 36

The Altitude 36 is the trail breaker of Tubbs's Altitude Series, with a deck area of 10″×36″ and a pair weight of 5.2 pounds. Rated at "over 200 pounds," this 'shoe easily carried 250 pounds (me plus backpack) over every type of terrain encountered. Like all the larger trail-buster models, it's a little more trouble to

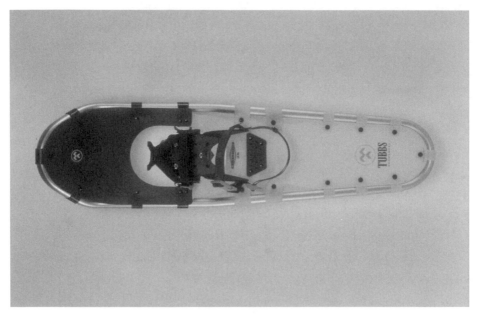

The Tubbs Altitude 10"x36" snowshoe.

The Tubbs TD91 binding.

manipulate in thick swamp, but balance and maneuverability are still very good, and flotation is of course excellent.

Much of the Altitude's easy handling can be attributed to Tubbs's patented TD91 Control Wing binding, which proved to be as secure as any I've used. The TD91's best advantage, I think, is a single instep strap that fastens with a quick-release buckle. This allows you to insert the toe of your boot under the toe straps until it fits snugly, then pull up the heel strap tight and secure the binding by simply snapping the preadjusted instep strap together. This makes getting the Altitudes on and off much quicker and more convenient than most other bindings.

My one complaint about the Altitude had to do with its tough Arc-Tec decking material. This heavy plastic sheeting is rugged and abrasion resistant enough to be called indestructible, but on crusted hardpack it makes loud scraping noises with every step. Someone likened the sound to an empty milk jug being kicked across the snow. On powder the Altitude was as quiet as any other 'shoe, but noise alone makes me opt for a different type of decking when the trail is over glazed snow.

TUBBS QUEST

This is the snowshoe that really rekindled interest in walking on snow. Many old-time snowshoers had regarded the shiny new synthetic models with distrust, fearful that aluminum frames might break under stress, plastic binding buckles might crack from subzero cold, or that Hypalon decking would tear. The 9"×30" Quest dispelled all doubts with a superstrong design that encases its stout aluminum frame in molded polyurethane.

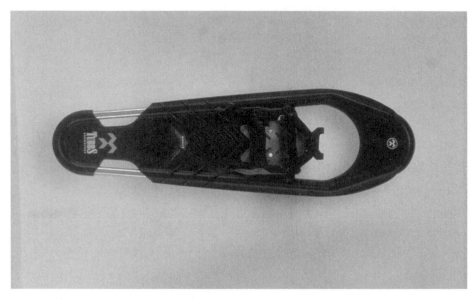

The Tubbs Quest 9"x30" snowshoe.

Rated to "180 pounds and over," the 9"×30" Quest proved un-breakable in more than 200 miles of backcountry 'shoeing, though 180 pounds is probably an accurate rating for powder snow. Pair weight is an advertised 5.1 pounds, and Tubbs's Quick-Step binding is both secure and comfortable. Retail is about $130 for the 9"×30" model, making it a best buy among modern snowshoes.

Glossary of Snowshoeing Terms

AVALANCHE

A wave of snow that breaks loose from its own weight to slide downhill with sometimes devastating force, picking up trees, rocks, and more snow as it descends. Tall, steep hills and deep snows are a combination sure to prompt snowslides, and snowshoers should avoid any places that look suspect.

BINDING

A flexible harness that holds a snowshoe snugly onto its wearer's feet with laces, straps, or buckles. A good and properly fitted binding makes the snowshoe an integral part of its wearer's foot, moving as it moves, with no lateral slop or looseness.

CLEAT

A sharp metal claw or spike that protrudes from the bottom of a snowshoe directly under the wearer's foot to provide sure traction on icy surfaces. See Crampon.

CORNICE

An undercut and sometimes curled-over drift of windblown snow usually found atop windswept ridges and ledges. Though often beautifully sculptured, when the snow on top of the undercut exceeds the weight it can support, the cornice will break loose and slide downhill, perhaps causing an avalanche.

CRAMPON

A cleat, usually aluminum or stainless steel, positioned to point downward on the binding under the ball and heel of a wearer's foot. Not to be confused with mountaineering crampons, snowshoe crampons provide sure footing on steep hills and ice too slippery to be negotiated safely by previous generations of snowshoes.

DEAD AIR

Warm, motionless air trapped within the fibers of a garment worn between the body and a windproof outer shell. Like the attic of a well-insulated house, these dead-air spaces retain body heat while dissipating perspiration vapors.

DECKING

The material used to span a snowshoe's frame, usually a crisscross lacing of leather or neoprene on traditional wooden-frame models, or a tough, continuous fabirc like Hypalon on modern shoes. Decking provides the surface area and flotation necessary to distribute a walker's weight and keep him on top of the snow.

DENIER

A logarithmic scale used to determine the coarseness or fineness of silk and synthetic yarns and threads, based on a standard of 50 milligrams of weight per 450 meters of thread. In general, the higher the denier value, the lighter the thread used and the denser the fabric made from it; heavier threads result in a more coarse fabric with a lower denier value.

FLOTATION

The ability of a snowshoe to distribute and support its wearer's weight on snow, especially powder. Generally, flotation increases with the surface area of a snowshoe, because larger surface area results in better weight displacement and less downward force per square inch than with smaller shoes.

FRAME

A continuous loop of wood, aluminum, or composite material across which a snowshoe's decking and binding are mounted. The frame is the strength of the snowshoe, and it should be as near unbreakable as possible.

FROSTBITE

A damaging and potentially serious exposure to cold in which skin freezes, turning white as moisture in living flesh crystalizes into ice. In extreme cases frostbite completely kills affected tissues; gangrene may result, sometimes necessitating amputation of entire limbs.

HARDPACK

A base layer of snow that has been compacted under its own weight, reducing what had been, say, 6 feet of fluff to perhaps 2 feet of hardpack snow.

MUKLUK

A Native American–style soft-sole winter boot, very much like a moccasin but ankle or knee high with long laces that wrap around and help support the ankles. Despite having no arch support, a mukluk's pliable sole helps keep its wearer's feet warm by exercising the soles and maximizing blood flow.

NESTING

A feature of wide-frame, usually traditional-style, snowshoes in which the tail radius of the forward snowshoe mates precisely with the outside radius of the rearward 'shoe's toe. This permits the wearer to walk with a narrower, less bowlegged stance than would be possible if the 'shoes were placed directly side by side. Length of stride is also dictated by where the 'shoes nest, so potential buyers or renters should always put on a pair of snowshoes and check to see if their respective stride lengths are comparable.

PARKA SHELL

An uninsulated, windproof, and preferably waterproof hooded jacket of densely woven material that negates windchill. Removing the shell during periods of heavy exertion allows insulating layers worn beneath it to dissipate perspiration.

PAC BOOT

An insulated winter boot, usually with a removable liner that can be dried or replaced as needed.

POWDER

Fresh, fluffy, often drifted snow. Powder is the softest and usually most tiring type of snow on which to break trail.

SNOWSLIDE

See Avalanche.

QUICK-RELEASE

A type of buckle, usually plastic, found on most modern snowshoe bindings. These buckles tighten by pulling on the loose end of the binding strap, release by pushing the rear of the buckle upward with a thumb, and often unclip to separate a strap entirely.

TRACKING

The tendency of a snowshoe to follow its wearer's foot as he steps forward. A snowshoe whose tail drags straight behind, with no lateral play or looseness, is easier to walk on and less tiring.

TRANSVERSE

A crosswise route that angles upward or downward diagonally across the face of a slope too steep to climb or descend from directly. With this method, the snowshoe frame's edges are used to cut and pack steps into the hill's face. Synthetic snowshoes with crampon bindings usually provide sufficient traction to take hills head-on from either direction.

VOIDS

Sometimes large, hollow areas concealed beneath solid-looking hardpack snow that has accumulated on top of, but not below, dense brush. Supported only by the springy branches of river willows and dogwoods, voids can cave in under a snowshoer's weight. They pose a hazard especially around lakeshores and riverbanks.

WHITEOUT

A curtain of wind-driven snow so dense that it can limit visibility to just a few feet, and usually accompanied by windchills far below zero. Whiteouts are encountered at wide-open places like prairies, frozen lakes, and large tracts of deforested flatland, and so are generally easy for a snowshoer to avoid by staying inside the tree line.

Snowshoe Manufacturers

The following list of snowshoe manufacturers should prove helpful to those wishing to compare models before purchasing a new set of snowshoes. Inclusion on this list does not represent an endorsement by the author.

Atlas Snow-Shoe Company
1830 Harrison Street
San Francisco, CA 94103
Telephone: (415) 703-0414
Website: www.atlasworld.com/

Great Bear Enterprises
P.O. Box 428
Kila, MT 59920
Telephone: (406) 257-6992 or (877) 296-2330
Contact: Ron Amos
Website: www.shopworks.com

Iverson Snowshoe Company
P.O. Box 85
FB—Maple Street
Shingleton, MI 49884
Telephone: (906) 452-6370
Fax: (906) 452-6480
Website: www.iversonsnowshoe.com/

Little Bear Snowshoes
A Division of Spring Brook Manufacturing.
2477 I Road
Grand Junction, CO 81505
Telephone: (800) 655-8984 or (970) 241-8546
Website: www.springbrook.com

Mountain Safety Research (MSR), Inc.
P.O. Box 24547
Seattle, WA 98124
Telephone: (800) 877-9677
Fax: (206) 682-4184
Website: www.msrcorp.com

Northern Lites Snowshoes
1300 Cleveland
Wausau, WI 54401
Telephone: (800) 360-5483
Website: www.northernlites.com/

Wing Enterprises, Inc.
1325 West Industrial Circle
Springville, UT 84663-3100
Telephone: (800) 453-1192
Website: www.powderwings.com

Prater Snowshoes
3740 Cove Road
Ellensburg, WA 98926
Telephone: (509) 925-1212
Website: www.adsnet.net/prater/

Redfeather Design, Inc.
4955-D Peoria Street
Denver, CO 80239
Telephone: (800) 525-0081
E-mail: rfsnowshoe@earthlink.net

Sherpa Snowshoe Company
P.O. Box 607
Milwaukee, WI 53201-0607
Telephone: (800) 621-2277
Website: www.sherpasnowshoes.com

Tubbs Snowshoe Company
52 River Road
Stowe, VT 05672
Telephone: (800) 882-2748 or (802)253-7398
Website: www.tubbssnowshoes.com

Snowshoeing Destinations Directory

While even snowbound urban areas usually offer lots of un-tracked snow to walk over, sooner or later everyone who gets snow-shoeing into his blood will experience a yen to try his skills in a wilderness setting. It's usually a lot easier for busy people, and especially those who live in places that lack snow, to plan a snow-shoeing trip when they have an idea of where to go in their area and who to call for more information.

The following directory of snowshoeing destinations should help eliminate some of that confusion, but always be sure to call ahead for the most current information about local weather and trail conditions. If your intended destination isn't listed here, the local chamber of commerce, conservation department field office, or even ski resorts in the area are also good sources of snowshoeing information.

Wherever you elect to snowshoe, remember to go prepared, stay warm, and, above all, bring your camera and binocular.

ALASKA:

Chugach State Park
Potter Section House and Chugach State Park Headquarters
Mile 115, Seward Highway
H.C. 52, Box 8999
Indian, AK 99540
Phone: (907) 345-5014
Fax: (907) 345-6982
Trails: Ship Creek Valley, Bird Creek Trail, Bold Ridge
    Trail, Eklutna Lakeside Trail, Glen Alps Trailhead,
    Middle Fork Loop Trail, Crow Pass (Iditarod) Trail

Denali National Park
P.O. Box 9
Denali National Park, AK 99755
Phone: (907) 683-2294
Trails: Mount Healy Overlook Trail, Taiga Loop Trail

Juneau Recreation Area
Forest Service Information Center
Centennial Hall
101 Egan Drive
Juneau, AK 99801
Phone: (907) 586-8751 or (907) 586-5226 (after 4:30 P.M.)
Trails: Weekly snowshoe tours November through April

Kenai National Wildlife Refuge
Box 2139
Soldotna, AK 99669
Phone: (907) 262-7021
Fax: (907) 262-3599
Trails: Seven Lakes, Kenai River, Funny River, Bear

Creek, Moose Creek, Fuller Lake, Cottonwood Creek, Lake Emma, McKinley Lake, Resurrection Pass, Carter Lake, Lost Lake

Wrangell–St. Elias National Park
P.O. Box 29
Glennallen, AK 99588
Phone: (907) 822-5235

Nabesna Ranger Station
P.O. Box 885
Slana, AK 99586
Phone: (907) 822-5238

Chitina Ranger Station
P.O. Box 110
Chitina, AK 99566
Phone: (907) 823-2205

Yatutat Ranger Station
P.O. Box 137
Yakutat, AK 99689
Phone: (907) 784-3295
Trails: Dixie Pass–Kotsina Trail Loop, Goodlata Peak, Lost Creek Trail, Nugget Creek Trail, Soda Lake Trail, Tanada Lake Trail

COLORADO:

Black Canyon of the Gunnison National Park
102 Elk Creek
Gunnison, CO 81230
Phone: (970) 641-2337

Curecanti National Recreation Area
102 Elk Creek
Gunnison, CO 81230-9304
Phone: (970) 641-2337

Florissant Fossil Beds National Monument
P.O. Box 185
Florissant, CO 80816-0185
Phone: (719) 748-3253

Grand Sand Dunes National Monument
11500 Highway 150
Mosca, CO 81146-9798
Phone: (719) 378-2312

Mesa Verde National Park
P.O. Box 8
Mesa Verde, CO 81330-0008
Phone: (970) 529-4465

Rocky Mountain National Park
Estes Park, CO 80517-8397
Phone: (970) 586-1206

INDIANA:

Indiana Dunes National Lakeshore
1100 North Mineral Springs Road
Porter, IN 46304-1299
Phone: (219) 926-7561
Trails: Ly-Co-Ki-We

MICHIGAN:

Hiawatha National Forest:
>   Munising District
>   Rt 2, Box 400
>   Munising, MI 49862
>   Phone: (906) 387-3700

>   St. Ignace District
>   1498 West U.S. 2
>   St. Ignace, MI 49781
>   Phone: (906) 643-7900

>   Rapid River District
>   8181 U.S. 2
>   Rapid River, MI 49878
>   Phone: (906) 474-6442

Huron-Manistee National Forests
Michigan Department of Natural Resources
P.O. Box 77
Newberry, MI 49868
Phone: (906) 293-5131
Trails: Algonquin Pathway, Canada Lakes Pathway, Giant
    Pines Loop, Indian Lake Pathway, Pine Bowl Pathway

Pictured Rocks National Lakeshore
P.O. Box 40
Munsing, MI 49862-0040
Phone: (906) 387-3700
Trails: Munising Falls, Sand Point, Cliffs Group Site, Miners
    Castle, Potato Patch, Mosquito River, Chapel Falls, Coves
    Group Site, Beaver Creek, Pine Bluff, Trappers Lake Trail,

7 Mile Creek, 12 Mile Beach, Benchmark, Au Sable Point
East, Log Slide, Masse Homestead, Grand Sable

Seney National Wildlife Refuge
H.C.R. 2, Box 1
Seney, MI 49883
Phone: (906) 586-9851

Sleeping Bear Dunes National Lakeshore
9922 Front St.
Empire, MI 49630-9797
Phone: (616) 326-5134
Trails: Alligator Hill Trail, Bay View Trail, Empire Bluff Trail,
    Good Harbor Bay Trail, Old Indian Trail, Platte Plains
    Trail, Pyramid Point Trail, Shauger Hill Trail, Windy
    Moraine Trail

MINNESOTA:

Chippewa National Forest
Route 3, Box 244
Cass Lake, MN 56633
Phone: (218) 335-8673

Superior National Forest
P.O. Box 338, 515 West First Street
Duluth, MN 55802
Phone: (218) 720-5324

Kawishiwi Ranger District
Ely, MN
Phone: (218) 365-7600
Trails: Coxey Pond Trail, Slim Lake Trail

NEW HAMPSHIRE:

White Mountain National Forest
719 Main Street
Laconia, NH 03246-0772
Phone: (603) 528-8721 or (603) 447-5448
Trails: Approximately 600 miles of hiking trails that serve as
snowshoe trails in winter

OREGON:

Bear Springs District
Trails: Barlow Pass, Pioneer Trail, Pioneer Women's Grave
Trail, Barlow Ridge

Hood River District
Trails: Bennett Pass, Pocket Creek Trail, Robinhood Creek
Loop Trail, East Fork Hiking Trail

Zigzag District
Trails: Summit Trail, Glacier View Loop, Lolo Pass Loop,
Old Maid Flat Area, Trillium Lake Loop, Quarry Loop,
Westleg/Glade Trail, West Leg Trail, Yellow Jacket Trail

PENNSYLVANIA:

Blue Knob State Forest
R.R. 1, Box 449
Imler, PA 16655-9407
Phone: (814) 276-3576
Trails: Several; trail maps are available

Forbes State Forest
P.O. Box 519
Laughlintown, PA 15655

Phone: (412) 238-9533
Trails: Trail maps are available

Gallitzin State Forest
131 Hillcrest Drive
Edensburg, PA 15931
Phone: (814) 472-8320
Trails: Trail maps are available

Keystone State Park
R.R. 2, Box 101
Derry, PA 15627-9617
Phone: (412) 668-2939

Kooser State Park
R.R. 4, Box 256
Somerset, PA 15501-8509
Phone: (814) 445-8673 (park office)
Trails: A single short (1.5-mile) groomed trail

Laurel Ridge State Park
R.R. 3, Box 246
Rockwood, PA 15557-8703
Phone: (412) 455-3744 (park office) or (412) 455-7303
Trails: One located on the top of Laurel Mountain

Moraine State Park
R.R. 1, Box 212
Portersville, PA 16051-9650
Phone: (412) 368-8811
Trails: Several, marked and groomed

Ohiopyle State Park
P.O. Box 105
Ohiopyle, PA 15470-0105
Phone: (412) 329-8591
Trails: Youhgiogheny River Gorge, Jonathan Run,
    Cucumber Run

Prince Gallitzin State Park
R.R. 1, Box 79
Patton, PA 16668-9201
Phone: (814) 674-1000
Trails: One, marked

Raccoon Creek State Park
3000 State Route 18
Hookstown, PA 15050-9416
Phone: (412) 899-2200
Trails: Raccoon Creek Trail

Ryerson Station State Park
R.R. 1, Box 77
Wind Ridge, PA 15380-9733

UTAH:

Ashley National Forest
Vernal Ranger District
355 N. Vernal Ave.
Vernal, UT 84078
Phone: (801) 789-1181
Trails: Bassett Springs Loop Trail, Bear Canyon–Bootleg Trail,
    Canyon Rim Trail, Swett Ranch Loop

Bryce Canyon National Park
Bryce Canyon, UT 84717-0001
Phone: (435) 834-5322

Manti–La Sal National Forest
Moab Ranger District
125 West 200 South
Moab, UT 84532
Phone: (801) 259-7155
Trails: Trail maps are available

Wasatch-Cache National Forest
8230 Federal Building
125 S. State St.
Salt Lake City, UT 84138
Phone: (801) 524-5030
Trails: North Ogden Trailhead, Mount Ogden, Liberty-Avon
    Road, James Peak Trailhead, Mantua-Willard Basin,
    Mantua Trailhead, Monte Cristo Area, Snow Basin,
    North Fork Park, Maples Campground, Sardine Ridge,
    Browns Hole, Wheatgrass Canyon, Causey Trailhead

Zion National Park
Springdale, UT 84767
Phone: (435) 772-3256

VERMONT:

Green Mountain and Finger Lakes National Forests
231 North Main Street
Rutland, VT 05701-2417
Phone: (802) 747-6709
Trails: Lake Pleiad, Mt. Moosalamoo, Rattlesnake Cliffs,
    Aunt Jenny Trail

WISCONSIN:

Chequamegon National Forest
1170 4th Avenue South
Park Falls, WI 54552
Phone: (715) 762-5175
Trails: Black Lake Trail

Medford District Ranger USDA-Forest Service
850 North 8th , Highway 13
Medford, WI 54451
Phone: (715) 748-4875
Trails: Part of a 600-mile trail system

Washburn Ranger District
USDA—Forest Service
P.O. Box 578
Washburn, WI 54891
Phone: (715) 573-2667
Fax: (715) 373-2878
Trails: North Country Scenic Trail

Nicolet National Forest
68 South Stevens Street
Rhinelander, WI 54501-3496
Phone: (715) 362-1354
Trails: Hiking trails, seasonal roads

WEST VIRGINIA:

Monongahela National Forest
200 Sycamore Street
Elkins, WV 26241-3962
Phone: (304) 636-1800

Cheat Ranger District
P.O. Box 368
Parsons, WV 26287
Phone: (304) 478-3251
Trails: Canaan Mountain Area, Canyon Rim Area,
    Stuart Memorial Drive

Gauley Ranger District
Box 110
Richwood, WV 26261
Phone: (304) 846-2695

Greenbrier Ranger District
Box 67
Bartow, WV 24920
Phone: (304) 456-3335
Trails: Shavers Fork Area, Cheat Mountain, Old Spruce Area,
    Middle Mountain Area

Marlinton Ranger District
P.O. Box 210
Marlinton, WV 24954-0210
Phone: (304) 799-4334
Trails: Highland Scenic Highway, Cranberry Mountain
    Nature Center

Potomac Ranger District
H.C. 59, Box 240
Petersburg, WV 26847
Phone: (304) 257-4488
Trails: Dolly Sods, Spruce Knob Area

Index